Historic
Railway Sites
in Britain

Overleaf: *Eynsford Viaduct*

Historic
Railway Sites
in Britain

MICHAEL R. BONAVIA

Robert Hale Limited
Clerkenwell House
Clerkenwell Green
London EC1R 0HT

British Library Cataloguing in Publication Data

Bonavia, Michael R.
   Historic railway sites in Britain.
   1. Railroads — Great Britain
   2. Industrial archaeology — Great
   Britain
   I. Title
   625.1'00941   TF57

   ISBN 0-7090-3156-4

Photoset in Ehrhardt by
Derek Doyle & Associates, Mold, Clwyd
Printed in Great Britain by
St Edmundsbury Press Ltd, Bury St Edmunds, Suffolk
Bound by WBC Bookbinders Ltd.

Contents

For Kethi

List of Illustrations

Foreword

by David Shepherd

When I was training to be an artist I was told always to look around me and 'notice things'. Awareness of one's surroundings, whether man-made or natural, surely adds to the fulfilment of life.

Michael Bonavia's book is not another railway book, for railway enthusiasts. This enlightening book is for those who make the effort to appreciate how rich Britain is in railway architecture, whether it be the ultimate example of Victorian extravagance – St Pancras Station – or the architectural detail of a bridge buried in the depths of the countryside across which trains have long ceased to run; for this country, the birthplace of steam railways, has untold riches to discover, appreciate and ponder over.

As Michael says in his book, there were bursts of railway mania at certain periods during the last century when England, it seemed, would be covered in a tangle of branch lines; one small market town possibly having three competing railway companies rushing to get at it, and all of them probably going bust in the process within a short period of time. Nevertheless, the Victorians did things with relish. They were not prepared, as we are today, in this ugly functional age, to put up a faceless slab of concrete and call it a bridge. They embellished it with the company crest in the fancy cast-ironwork. The man who designed that bridge was not just an engineer, he was an artist. The Victorians were not content to put up bus shelters made of plywood and call them stations. When Brunel put a railway through a hillside, he was not just content to build a tunnel. He embellished the tunnel mouth to look like a castle. He was proud of his prowess as an artist and he was not ashamed to say so.

In the emasculation of Britain's railways since World War II, so much has inevitably been lost. (We can't save everything; although the enthusiasts, of which I am proud to be one, have done their best – I bought a beautiful Victorian footbridge from British Rail for £10 to save it being smashed to pieces, but that is another story!) However, I believe now that we have turned the corner and realized that we cannot destroy these great and small masterpieces which represent the very best of Victorian railway architecture.

Within six miles of where I live there are two examples of the best and the worst. Indeed Michael refers in his book to the station in my own home town of Godalming. Here industry and British Rail have combined to restore completely the magnificence of the last century down to the minutest detail, even the gilt on the ceiling of the booking hall. In contrast a few miles away poor old Guildford Station has been hacked about mercilessly until it resembles a body without arms and legs; better to knock it down altogether and put up a 'shoebox'.

I have a great deal of sympathy now for British Rail. Their business is to run a railway in a country which in the past, and perhaps today also, does not altogether care about its railway system as much as it should. British Rail has been landed with an enormous number of buildings and structures which, because they are listed, cannot be pulled down. They are useless to British Rail and yet they still have the financial burden of upkeep. In the case of Bath Green Park Station, commerce has again come to the rescue. This magnificent structure was lifeless and ghostlike – cars stood in rows like so many coffins and pigeons fluttered in the roof of the great steam shed where steam trains lived and breathed. One of our big supermarket chains then came to the rescue and, whilst the steam trains have gone for ever, at least the station has been completely refurbished and has come to life, albeit in a different form.

I believe that everyone, when given the opportunity, should avoid the traffic-choked motorways and travel by train. There is no better way to look at the landscape. Michael's book is not only a joy to read, it also does a great service and every traveller by train should have a copy with them. They will be rewarded.

D.S.

General Introduction

Although Britain obtained a comprehensive railway network earlier and more quickly than any other European country, construction did not proceed at an even pace. There were great bursts of enthusiasm for railway promotion, with quieter periods intervening. First came the two 'railway manias', in the 1830s and 1840s, followed by a third era of rapid expansion after the middle of the century, only briefly checked by the financial crisis of 1866.

There was, however, a significant difference between the philosophies of the earlier and later construction periods. The novelty of steam railroads fired many imaginations and led, in the early years, to a grandiose view of what the new systems should look like, in terms both of engineering and of architecture. It produced the Euston Arch or 'Propylaeum' and the impressive and ornate structures built by Brunel for the Great Western Railway; and, all along the lines, many charming stations in a classical or neo-Gothic idiom, as well as strikingly decorative tunnel entrances and bridges.

Later, a cooler financial outlook, based upon a more realistic appraisal of the railways' potential and limitations, appeared. Major construction was now often undertaken to protect or improve a company's competitive position, and construction costs were scrutinized much more closely. Another factor was the increasing power of the steam locomotive, which enabled even the main lines to be built with gradients steeper than had previously been considered acceptable. That in turn reduced somewhat the need for the massive earthworks and structures so characteristic of the first trunk routes. The London and Birmingham Railway, opened in 1838, had a 'ruling gradient' of 1 in 330; the Great Northern, opened in 1850, 1 in 200; the Midland's London extension, opened in 1868, 1 in 176 – 1 in 200.

By 1870 the main railway network was virtually complete; the route mileage had reached just over 11,000. Later additions comprised mainly branches and 'infilling', with also a very few main lines, such as the Great Central's London extension, opened in 1899. The peak was reached in the twentieth century: at nationalization in 1948, the mileage totalled over 19,600. The present-day, post-Beeching total has fallen to about 10,500 miles.

Very significant for the study of historic railway sites is the reduction in the number of stations open to traffic. From the immediate pre-nationalization total of 8,294 (taking passenger and goods stations together) there has been a dramatic fall to about 2,600. What has happened to all these redundant buildings? Some have been sold and adapted as private dwellings or for commercial use; some have been demolished; others remain awaiting disposal, boarded up and a target for vandalism.

To summarize the visual aspects resulting from this long history of expansion followed by contraction: what we see today results mainly from the fact that the greater part of the railways' infrastructure – stations and major civil engineering works – was built at a time when architectural fashions were changing fast. The orthodox classical styles which had dominated the eighteenth century had already encountered opposition from practitioners of the neo-Gothic. But the latter style expressed itself first in smaller works such as stations and stationmasters' houses, often built as *cottages ornés* with gables and mullions, rather than in the massive terminal buildings of the 1840s and 1850s, some of which suggested Graeco-Roman palaces. A post-Renaissance 'Italianate' style, with round-headed windows, pantiles and sometimes a kind of *campanile*, also appeared here and there, notably at London Bridge Station. Massive neo-Gothic works (the archetype of which is the St Pancras Hotel) appeared rather later, having been sometimes elbowed out by a romantic Victorian re-creation of Elizabethan or Jacobean mannerisms, such as at Bristol (Temple Meads).

One can perhaps summarize the growth of railway architectural style as a turning-away, as the nineteenth century progressed, from reliance upon well-tried classical formulae into the eclecticism characteristic of Victorian art, in which almost every cliché of past styles could be incorporated.

The role of the architect in the design of early railway stations and other structures is not always clear, least of all as regards the relationship between the all-powerful engineer and the architect. Some engineers, like Brunel (who was a polymath, almost a nineteenth-century Leonardo da Vinci), designed houses and station buildings themselves. This was not confined to the early years: as late as the 1860s, the Chief Engineer of the Great Eastern Railway, Edward Wilson, personally designed the buildings for the new

St Pancras Hotel building, masking the impressive train shed behind; the apotheosis of the mid-Victorian Gothic revival

Liverpool Street terminus. The Great Central Railway's Marylebone terminus was also designed by that railway's Chief Engineer – probably to economize on architect's fees!

Well into the twentieth century, the Great Western Railway, following the Brunel tradition, showed a strong preference for doing everything possible as an 'in-house' operation. (There is a story that the Great Western Royal Hotel once found itself short of ashtrays, so an order was sent to Swindon Works; which in due course despatched a consignment of these useful articles – in solid cast-iron and displaying the company's arms, almost too heavy to lift.) In any case, the names of outside architects are seldom to be found where ex-GWR buildings are concerned.

On the other hand, in very early days Robert Stephenson engaged an outside architect to help him realize an Egyptian character in the towers for his monumental Menai Bridge. Many early railways prided themselves on engaging the best contemporary architectural talent.

British Rail's encyclopedia of DoE-listed railway buildings identifies some seventy-five architects known (or, in some cases, believed) to have been employed. Their status seems to have varied considerably. At one extreme, the Midland Railway employed Sir Gilbert Scott (1811-78), probably the best-known (and most expensive) architect of his generation, for a one-off job, the Midland Grand Hotel at St Pancras. Several railways had earlier employed Sir William Tite (1798-1873), who had an enormous practice, to design many stations as far apart as Carlisle and the South of England. At the other extreme is the rather shadowy figure of Francis Thompson, about whom relatively little is known, though his stations for the North Midland Railway, the Eastern Counties Railway and the Chester & Holyhead Railway are all excellent, well-mannered designs. Crediting the actual authorship of designs between architects is sometimes difficult – for example at Cambridge, between Sancton Wood and Francis Thompson.

The lot of the Railway Company's architect has not always been easy since, in addition to special site problems, the requirements of the traffic departments and of the civil engineer could be exacting. In recent times the scope for new designs by architects has been limited, since new railway construction has been rare. And the dominant position of the engineer in the past has sometimes had unfortunate effects; repairs and extensions effected by district engineers, to what originally were well-balanced and attractive buildings, were too often carried out crudely, showing a regrettable insensitivity – for example, using brickwork to patch stonework. This even happened to some of Brunel's work at Bath, surprisingly for the GWR which seldom seemed penny-pinching. This is fortunately less common in British Rail today, though shortage of funds minimizes the amount of preservation or restoration that can be carried out. In some cases either local authorities or private firms can help: for instance, Godalming Station in Surrey has been sympathetically renovated with a grant from a local brewery. One must hope for many more such cases.

It cannot be too strongly emphasized that things are constantly changing in this field of interest. Since this book was started, the last portions of Broad Street Station in the City of London, once a busy terminus, have completely disappeared. On the other hand, Marylebone Station, then under threat of closure, has been indefinitely reprieved. British Rail's own former headquarters has been sold. But, almost every month, news comes in that another station somewhere is to be renovated; and the good news is that nowadays this frequently involves, essentially, restoration, rather than demolition and replacement by a practical but probably relatively uninteresting 'functional' structure.

British Rail's changing organization is not without effect upon buildings: the work of 'Network South-East' in brightening up passenger stations, admirable in principle, may lead to some loss of historical identity or, on the other hand, reveal some attractive features of the original design that had been obscured for years, such as ornamental cast-iron capitals to roof-supporting columns. Increasingly it is realized that sensitive restoration can often be no more expensive than demolition and rebuilding; organizations such as the Railway Heritage Trust offer awards for the best restored 'listed' railway structure.

The now demolished Broad Street Station dating from 1865, showing marked French influence

What actually constitutes an 'historic' site? British Rail's own survey of its architectural and engineering heritage lists over 385 structures which the Department of the Environment considers to be of special architectural or historic interest, and the list is regularly updated. There are also a number of railway buildings of historical or architectural importance that are no longer in BR ownership, such as Bath (Green Park) Station. Nor must one forget that some other transport undertakings own historic railway buildings. London's first Underground was opened in 1863, and London Regional Transport possesses a number of interesting buildings. The Metropolitan Railway, absorbed into the London Passenger Transport Board in 1933, had delighted to describe itself as 'a trunk line in miniature', and it handled goods and parcels traffic as well as passengers. Furthermore, some of the privately preserved railway societies have acquired stations and structures of significance, even though their prime object has been the restoration of steam locomotives and rolling stock, and running steam trains.

Faced with the breadth of the subject on the one hand and the constraints of space on the other, this book strikes a middle course which it is hoped will enlist the interest of many readers, while persuading some to go on to more specialized studies. In each of the chief regions of Great Britain a general introduction on the special railway interest of the area is followed by entries covering a representative selection of structures (stations, viaducts, tunnels, etc); these notes usually deal briefly with the history of each, as well as with its main architectural features, together with the name of the architect, if known. The choice of subjects is the author's, and therefore may not satisfy everyone; but any list claiming to be truly comprehensive would invite controversy over what was included and omitted, and would extend far beyond the limitations of space of this book. A note on the principal preserved railways is included in the Appendix.

The great majority of structures are still in the care of British Rail; a few, however, although sold, still retain their architectural and historical railway interest, and a selection is therefore included. And although railway buildings built later than the early part of this century have been generally omitted, an exception has been made in the case of London Transport. The inter-war years were a fruitful architectural period in the history of that undertaking.

Obviously, many sites can easily be located by consulting the British Rail timetable index and train tables. Some, especially on closed branches, are accessible only by road; in such cases the relevant

Ordnance Survey map number in the 1:50,000 series is given, together with hints, if necessary, for reaching the site or obtaining the best view of, for instance, a spectacular viaduct. Public access may in some cases be restricted.

1. Inner and Outer London

Introduction

Inner London   The chief historical railway sites in the central area of the metropolis are of course the terminal stations. British Rail had no fewer than fourteen of these until the demolition of Broad Street started in 1985. But some have lost their 'historical' character by being submerged in new commercial development – for example, Blackfriars and Holborn Viaduct. Others are about to experience drastic reconstruction, though there is now a much greater interest in preserving any special features of merit surviving from the original design than was the case until recently.

One important feature is the siting of these termini, roughly on the perimeter of an irregular boundary enclosing the central zone. London has no main railway station as a focal point, no *Hauptbahnhof* or *Gare Centrale* such as one finds on the Continent. There are several reasons for this. First, Britain's railways were built by independent companies that were often strongly competitive and thus unwilling to join in the construction of a Union Station, such as were built in the USA – though, outside London, there were a few examples of this co-operation, notably in Carlisle, Manchester, Birmingham and Leeds. Second, the cost of land in the central London zone, and the concentration of its ownership in the hands of a few great estates, made site-acquisition difficult. Lastly and perhaps most importantly, Parliament early on showed itself unwilling to sanction main-line railway building within the area of Westminster and the whole West End of London, though subsequently some main lines from the south were permitted to bridge the Thames and obtain a foothold – nothing more – in the central area.

Some of the earliest stations to be built were sited inconveniently far from the centre. Paddington is an outstanding example, though it has never been replaced. However, the Shoreditch terminus of the Eastern Counties Railway, the Bricklayers' Arms and London Bridge Stations of the South Eastern Railway, and Nine Elms on the London

Modern Euston is functional but a last relic of the former station exists in the twin lodges in the Euston Road flanking the approach road

& South Western were all replaced by sites nearer the centre, though still right outside the West End.

Another factor in the proliferation of the London stations was the tremendous nineteenth-century growth in population (London expanded from 1.1 million in 1800 to 6.6 million in 1900). The process of station closure and reconstruction has therefore been prolonged, and not many stations have been exempt, though St Pancras is one example of a station that has been very little changed since it was first built. Those looking for historic sites will not find much to interest them in the new Euston — efficient and functional though it is. The same applies to those Southern Region stations that were most severely bomb-damaged during the 1939-45 war and which have been reconstructed as part of major office-development projects. Such schemes have provided much-needed improvement in the facilities for passengers but there is little remaining of historical interest at London Bridge, Cannon Street, Holborn Viaduct or Blackfriars. Just two relics remain: at Cannon Street the 'pepper-pots' at the end of the retaining walls enclosing the station have been restored, and at Blackfriars the carved stone list of destinations that could formerly be reached via the London Chatham and Dover Railway – with Westgate-on-Sea jostling St Petersburg, and Sevenoaks next to Lucerne – remains, though on a new site.

The major termini best deserving a visit therefore comprise St Pancras, King's Cross, Liverpool Street and Paddington. A few other railway sites in the central zone are also worth visiting.

Outer London   The growth in London's population during the nineteenth century and the appearance of a huge demand for commuter rail travel led to much building and rebuilding of stations in the whole area of Greater London, often involving the loss of original railway buildings of some charm. The emergence of a demand for residential daily travel had not been foreseen at the outset, when railways were viewed as essentially a form of long-distance travel, replacing the stage-coach, not the omnibus. It is extraordinary to recall that when the London & Birmingham Railway was opened in 1838, the first station out from the London terminus was at Harrow, $11\frac{1}{2}$ miles away. Thirty years later, however, the companies south of the Thames were competing fiercely for the daily residential traveller, promoting a whole network of lines and stations. Among these second-generation railways, interesting relics of the early Railway Age are not easy to find. London suburbs do, however, boast at least one spectacular railway viaduct and a few stations that retain some of their pristine character. There are also some modern buildings of merit owned by London Regional Transport.

A station converted into a museum exists at North Woolwich; it commemorates the Great Eastern Railway following its rescue by the Passmore Edwards Museum Trust. Other station buildings which have become surplus to railway needs and have been adapted for other purposes include Denmark Hill in South London – in which case a disastrous fire had taken place and BR could see no justification for restoring the original building, whereas a commercial use (as a pub) could be found for it after renovation work by a group of bodies interested in preservation. The work attracted a Civic Trust award.

St Pancras Station

St Pancras, much criticized and much praised, is a 'must' for anyone interested in Britain's railway heritage. The builders were the Midland Railway men who had formerly had to send their trains to London by exercising statutory 'running powers' over the Great Northern's line into King's Cross, and had seen their own traffic always delayed in favour of that of the owning company. They took their revenge by building their own line into London with a terminus next door to that of their erstwhile host, dominating it with a huge train shed and a stupendous hotel building. Gilbert Scott's apotheosis of the Gothic Revival and the sheer imaginative fantasy of this architect have as much power to impress today as when the building arose in all its brash newness to surprise London, with completion in 1873.

To see St Pancras at its best, one should climb half-way up the hill along the Pentonville Road. There is a celebrated view of the station from this point painted by John O'Connor in 1881, a romantic picture of Victorian London which can hardly be bettered. As a correspondent wrote to *The Times* on 12 September 1966, 'Whatever one may feel about St Pancras as a work of art, no one can deny that its presence is powerful, not least as a grand symbol of what, for all its faults, was one of the greatest periods in this island's history.'

The architect's skill in using this elevated site, with the great curving wing of the hotel at the west end and the long ramp leading to the east side entrance, cannot be denied even by those who are allergic to the Gothic Revival. The station's booking-office, with its oak panelling, particularly deserves inspection. Sadly, the hotel building has long been closed to the public; it ceased to accommodate guests as long ago as 1935, when the LMS Railway found it uneconomic and turned it into offices. Much of the splendid interior has been ruined and at the same time it has been found most unsuitable by its occupants, the office workers.

The 'Midland Grand Hotel', to give it its full name, has successively been subject to adulation, denigration and (today) general critical appreciation. Soon after it was opened, the historian of the Midland Railway wrote effusively that, 'It is a veritable railway palace ... the spacious and lofty apartments, the handsome furniture, the Brussels carpets, the massive silken or woollen curtains and the pinoleum blinds ... leave nothing to be desired by the wealthiest and the most refined.' Another writer declared, 'It is certainly the most sumptuous and the best conducted hotel in the empire.' It was placed under the management of a Mr Etzensberger (Swiss, no doubt) who had previously had charge of the catering on the Nile steamers 'as far as the first cataract'; this was apparently a great catering accolade – presumably the meals were less elaborate beyond the cataract!

One writer has called the hotel 'a great Gothic phantasmagoria'; some architects praise it highly, others have disliked it, but no one can ignore it. It is sad that the difficulty of modernizing it (for instance, by providing a bathroom for each bedroom) at an acceptable level of cost, long defeated catering organizations which considered taking it over.

At the time of writing, however, a firm proposal is on foot to

Details of capital to a column in the booking hall at St Pancras

restore the building – which has a Grade I listing – as an hotel at a cost of around £26 million. In Sir Peter Parker's time as Chairman of British Rail, the cleaning of the brickwork was put in hand, restoring it to virtually the appearance of newness after more than a century's weathering. Sadly, the work stopped half-way, presumably owing to financial stringency, leaving the frontage in a curious two-tone state. Development may at last see the work completed.

Behind the hotel is another masterpiece which is universally admired: the great train shed with its single span of 240 feet – forty feet more than the two spans of King's Cross put together – and its slightly pointed arch that echoes so well Gilbert Scott's Gothic hotel building. The designer of this splendid work was W.H. Barlow, the Consulting Engineer of the Midland Railway. Today, repainted, with the brickwork of the interior sidewalls and the glazing cleaned, it looks far fresher than it did formerly. In its present cleanliness it may even lack a little of the romance it had when clouds of steam wreathed the upper area and when the engines' blast as trains departed used to echo through the huge cavern.

The tie-bars of this great arch are located below the platforms and tracks; underneath the passenger station there was formerly quite a large goods station devoted to the Burton beer traffic, wagons for which were lowered or lifted by means of a hoist at the end of Platforms 3 and 4. A large Shire horse used to draw the wagons on and off the hoist with great skill and precision.

The undercroft of brick arches also housed a number of potato merchants at one time. The whole basement area, although not visible from the street, is being re-planned; the idea at the time of writing is to open it up as a car-park and retail shopping centre.

Enjoy St Pancras at all times, but particularly perhaps when shafts of sunlight, streaming through the mullioned windows of the booking office bring to mind J.B. Priestley's description of St Pancras as the most cathedral-like of stations. Anyone who wishes to delve more deeply into the history of this monument to Victorian ideology should read Professor Jack Simmons' *St Pancras Station*, an erudite but also entertaining book by a great authority.

King's Cross Station

There could be no greater contrast than that between King's Cross and its flamboyant neighbour, St Pancras. 'The Cross', as railwaymen call it, is an almost puritanical building from the architectural point of view, severe in the simplicity of its two arches, framed in yellow brick. The thrifty Yorkshire businessmen who financed the building of the Great Northern Railway to London were pleased to get a useful terminus at King's Cross for less, they alleged, than the £35,000 cost of the ornamental Doric arch (the 'Propylaeum') down the road at Euston. Lewis Cubitt (1799-1883). the architect, constructed two train sheds, allegedly on the model of the Tsar's riding school in Russia, following the then common principle of a single departure platform with passenger facilities along its entire length, and an arrival platform flanked by a cab road. In between were carriage sidings, connected by an intricate system of turntables by which the short, light carriages of the time could be manhandled by porters and marshalled into trains.

King's Cross with the simplicity of the original twin train sheds set off by a well-designed single-storey modern block

Today, of course, the whole space of the train sheds is occupied by platforms as well as tracks; but one can still observe the lightness of the structure and its suitability for its purpose. This has led in recent years to abandoning the idea, prevalent for a long time, of rebuilding 'The Cross'; instead, the brickwork has been cleaned and the scruffy 'African village' of shops and booths that long disfigured the frontage has been replaced by a glazed single-storey concourse that fills a long-felt need, while allowing Lewis Cubitt's façade to remain well appreciated.

The train shed and original 'Cubitt' frontage are listed buildings, Grade I. The new, necessary but utilitarian single-storey projection was given planning approval only for a limited period, due to expire in 1992.

BR has had further development proposals in mind, but these have been deferred partly on account of more recent listing of the hotel building (Grade II), the limited planning authority for the projecting concourse area and also the possibility that, when the Snow Hill link from Blackfriars Bridge to the Metropolitan 'widened lines' has been electrified, the closed 'Hotel Curve' tunnel, which does in fact pass under the hotel, might have to be reinstated.

Just as, beneath St Pancras, the electrified Midland Line trains are to run via Farringdon to the Southern Region over Blackfriars Bridge, there is the possibility of the closed connection between the widened lines and the Great Northern electrified system being reinstated. Some engineering work to accommodate the overhead electric conductor wire might be necessary in the tunnel beneath the hotel.

The hotel, now of course privately owned, was built soon after the station, in what is always described as an 'Italianate' style – a description applied equally to the Prince Consort's design for Osborne House and some of the pumping houses built by the Metropolitan Water Board. But the hotel is not aggressively 'Italianate'; the curve of the building is both ingenious and pleasing. Generations of travellers from the North have found the Great Northern Hotel a welcoming conclusion to their journey, only a stone's throw away from their arriving trains.

Liverpool Street Station

Liverpool Street Station is a creation of the mid-nineteenth century when the early concept of a terminus as needing just a departure platform (or 'parade') and an arrival platform had been overtaken by the growth of traffic and the need to provide more passenger facilities. The Great Eastern Railway (Eastern Counties until 1862) had originally built a terminus at Shoreditch, inconveniently far from the centre. In 1874 it came right into the City, with a new station at Liverpool Street, building what is today the main line station (Platforms 9 and 10) and (from 1875) the 'West Side suburban' platforms, 1 to 8. Although the station is not in its present state very satisfactory as an architectural entity, the great train shed is impressive, especially when sunlight streams through it. The best way to see Liverpool Street today is to walk the full length of the footbridge from the west end to Bishopsgate at the east end, noting the Art Deco style of the former west side tearoom on stilts at footbridge level, now housing the 'Europa Bistro'. A twin building on the east side was turned into the stationmaster's office a good many years ago.

Above the range of booking-office windows on the east bridge, careful scrutiny will reveal a series of delightful cherubs carved in the brickwork, each of whom is performing some railway task, firing a steam locomotive, waving a guard's flag or pulling a signal lever.

Overall, Liverpool Street is a less unified concept than most other stations; but it has its virtues and is a tribute to Edward Wilson, the Chief Engineer of the Great Eastern Railway, who, though not an architect, designed both the station and the 'subdued Gothic' railway offices. The ironwork of both the main line and west suburban train sheds is delicate and certainly justifies the statutory listing of the building. The east side, fronting Bishopsgate, built in 1894 with a girder type of glazed roof, is of less interest, apart from the 'cherub' reliefs mentioned above.

The adjacent Great Eastern Hotel, opened in 1884, was designed jointly by the son and grandson of Sir Charles Barry, the architect of the Houses of Parliament. But it is a far cry from the magnificent Gothic of Barry and Pugin at Westminster: the hotel's style has been described as 'vaguely Dutch Renaissance'. The banqueting suites called the Abercorn Rooms, facing Bishopsgate, were added in 1901 and are 'vaguely baroque' in character. They include two Masonic temples. They were built by another architect, Colonel R.W. Edis, who also built the Great Central Hotel adjoining Marylebone Station, which from 1948 to 1986 provided headquarters offices for the British Railways Board.

Liverpool Street is in the throes of a huge re-development scheme that will not be completed for several years. Until recently it had one feature in common with King's Cross: it was a low-level station with a high-level terminus of more flamboyant architectural character next door. Instead of St Pancras, Liverpool Street had as its neighbour Broad Street, built by the North London Railway. It stood on many brick arches and could be reached from street level only by a steep staircase. As at St Pancras, below the passenger station was a goods station to and from which wagons were transferred by hydraulic lifts.

Broad Street was actually an earlier arrival than its bigger neighbour, having been opened in 1865. It could hardly have been more French in character, with its mansard roof and turrets with decorative ironwork. From it a wide range of suburban services formerly ran, but it was very heavily damaged by bombing during the war, and neither the train services nor the building were substantially restored after the war. An atmosphere of semi-dereliction long pervaded the place, as its train services were gradually diverted elsewhere.

Broad Street was finally demolished in 1985-6, making room for the huge Broadgate development. This also embraces Liverpool Street, where – fortunately – the two fine arched train sheds covering Platforms 1 to 10 are to be preserved in the scheme; the less interesting, later section of the station Platforms 11 to 18, will be rafted over and major new buildings erected adjoining Bishopsgate. There will be a bonus for passengers in the shape of a redesigned concourse which will eliminate the awkward separation caused at present by the extension of the former main-line platforms (9 and 10) almost as far as the hotel, between the west and east suburban sides.

Liverpool Street Station, showing the truncated clock tower and the surviving 1875 frontage during the construction of the huge 'Broadgate' development

Nearly 150,000 passengers use this station daily, second only to Waterloo's 180,000, and many have cursed its inconvenient layout, when in a hurry.

Fenchurch Street Station

This is a curious place, even though the 65,000 commuters who hurry through it daily probably have little desire to pause and look around. The façade is remarkable for the big curved pediment topping the street frontage and the long saw-tooth awning below. The long windows are also worth noticing.

A big commercial development has transformed and modernized the rest of the station. The platforms have been rafted over and the concourse has been remodelled. However, as at other stations built above street level and approached by viaducts, passengers have to make a substantial ascent to reach the platforms.

Fenchurch Street has had a complex history. It started as the terminus of the London & Blackwall Railway, a system originally operated by cable traction and built to a non-standard gauge of five feet instead of 4 feet 8½ inches. The London & Blackwall was taken over by the Great Eastern; but meanwhile the North London Railway

The rather splendid façade of Fenchurch Street Station, masking the inconvenient access for passengers

used Fenchurch Street as its City terminus until after Broad Street was opened in 1865; by that time, yet another railway (the London, Tilbury & Southend line, absorbed by the Midland Railway in 1912) had entered Fenchurch Street and was eventually to monopolize the use of the station. This complicated history lends the place a certain interest even though today there are only the humdrum electric commuter trains to be seen at its platforms.

Fenchurch Street and Holborn Viaduct are the only main-line termini not served by London Transport trains as well as British Rail. Tower Hill on the Circle Line is the nearest Underground station to Fenchurch Street.

Charing Cross and Cannon Street Stations
These two stations were built in the 1860s by the South Eastern Railway, largely to counter the London, Chatham & Dover Railway's competitive thrust across the Thames into both the West End and the City of London. Originally they shared several features: each was sited at the end of a bridge over the Thames; each had an all-over barrel roof; and each was joined to the street by a large hotel building.

Charing Cross lost its barrel roof, designed by Sir John Hawkshaw, in 1905, when it collapsed, with several fatalities. The roof was rebuilt on a ridge-and-furrow pattern of steel girders. The principal changes since the station was built have been the disappearance of the 'cab road' that formerly emerged from a subway between two platforms; the modernization of the concourse and passenger facilities; and the severance of the connection between the station and the hotel.

In the courtyard between the Strand and the station stands the well-known reproduction Eleanor Cross, designed by the hotel's architect, E.M. Barry, when the hotel was built (1864). The original cross had stood some distance away and had been demolished in 1647. The Eleanor Crosses (originally twelve in all, of which only three survive) were erected by order of King Edward I in 1290 to mark the resting-places of the body of his Queen, Eleanor of Castile, on its journey from Lincoln to Westminster for burial. The reproduction cross is not necessarily authentic in detail, but it was based upon the design of the three surviving crosses on the funeral route.

The hotel is built in the 'French Renaissance' manner. The brick cladding of the rebuilt top storey detracts from the impressiveness of the building, which no longer belongs to British Rail – though its connection with the railway was close for over a century, above all during the years before 1914 when Charing Cross was London's principal Continental rail terminus. Distinguished travellers, including royalty, often stayed there.

Although the station's frontage is level with the Strand, the rapid slope of the ground down to the River Thames means that much of the station is built on arches which finally give way to the massive and unlovely Hungerford Railway Bridge spanning both the river and the Embankment. For many years the Player's Theatre has existed 'underneath the arches', as well as curio shops; there are plans to develop both the airspace above the platforms and the vaulted area beneath them for commercial purposes.

Cannon Street was built also by Hawkshaw, in quick succession to Charing Cross, and E.M. Barry provided an hotel of very similar design. The station closely resembled Charing Cross – though its barrel roof never collapsed like that at Charing Cross, but was destroyed through bombing in the Second World War. Cannon Street had a decorative feature lacking at Charing Cross, the 'pepper-pot' towers at the riverside end of the retaining walls. These survived the bombing and have recently been restored and cleaned; they are worth inspecting.

The Southern Railway found the Cannon Street Hotel to be

Cannon Street Station before complete redevelopment of the train shed area.
The turrets still stand, though the arched roof has gone

unsuccessful – surprisingly, since its only counterpart in the City of London was the rather similar, but financially successful, Great Eastern Hotel – and turned the building into offices, entitled Southern House, before the Second World War.

Following severe air-raid damage to Southern House and the station, reconstruction means that there is nothing left of the original buildings apart from the 'pepper-pots' and the side walls, to recall the days when all the principal trains to and from Charing Cross were worked via Cannon Street – a time-consuming reversal and a nightmare for the operating staff in charge of the junctions. Even so, and despite the drift westwards of so many business houses, Cannon Street still handles nearly 75,000 passengers daily, compared with Charing Cross's 120,000 or more.

Waterloo Station

Purists might consider that 'historic' is an inappropriate adjective to apply to Waterloo, since the station in its present form was completed as recently as 1922. But it has points of interest, because the modern station – spacious and convenient for passengers – is the product of a rebuilding that started in 1900 and continued for nearly a quarter of a century. The old station had been one of the most higgledy-piggledy affairs one can imagine: it was amusingly satirized by Jerome K. Jerome (himself a railwayman turned author) in *Three Men in a Boat*. Rebuilding took place in three stages, and even today one can just detect that there are still three stations under the clear roof-spans and the wide, unobstructed concourse: the south station (Platforms 1-4), the main line station (Platforms 5-15), and the Windsor station (Platforms 16-21). The brickwork of the last-named is quite different from that elsewhere.

The chief architectural feature of the station is the 'Victory Arch' at the top of a flight of steps leading down to York Road, with two large sculptured groups representing War and Peace. It was long known to the staff as 'pneumonia corner' on account of the piercing winds that blow up the staircase. Its notoriety in this respect was already established by the time King George V consented to perform the opening ceremony for the rebuilt station, on a day in March 1922. However, the King had a chill, the weather was inclement, and Queen Mary therefore performed the ceremony in his place.

In 1983 the discomforts of 'pneumonia corner' were much alleviated by the provision of an ornamental glass screen and glass doors within the arch, which also houses the Southern Railway's war memorial.

Recently, a new *terrazzo* flooring and general face-lifting of the station concourse have made Waterloo probably the most cheerful terminus in London. Its selection as the London terminus for train services through the projected Channel Tunnel will mean substantial alterations. 'Waterloo International' is planned to occupy the site of part of the present 'Windsor' side of the station, substantially extended at the outer extremity to allow space for a new concourse area with all the facilities usually associated with an airport.

It is intended to remodel the space occupied by Platforms 16-21 to provide 'International' platforms 1,097 feet long. New suburban platforms, partly on the site of the existing carriageway between Platforms 11 and 12, will handle the displaced traffic.

The passage-way from the main station to Waterloo (East) station utilizes a bridge that formerly carried a single line of railway that crossed the concourse of the main station and joined the former South Eastern Railway's line from Charing Cross. For many years, until its removal in 1985, a platform awning from the old link line remained in place, though the rails had long since been taken up and replaced by a footway. Even today, some old railwaymen still refer to

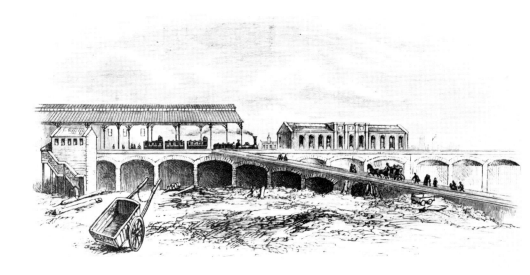

Waterloo Station, soon after it was first built in 1848, at the end of the extension line from Nine Elms

the eastern station as 'Waterloo Junction'. The junction was sometimes used in the nineteenth century for a few sporadic suburban train services but these soon disappeared, and thereafter its main use was for special trains, especially military specials to and from Aldershot, and for Queen Victoria's rail journeys from Windsor to Dover for the Continent. (The Queen spent more time on the Continent, especially in later life and in winter, than most of her subjects realized. Her journeys were very private.) The pedestrian way has now been modernized and brightened with several retail outlets on the bridge.

Waterloo main station was always well equipped in Southern Railway days with catering provided by, first, Spiers & Pond, and then Frederick Hotels. The Surrey Rooms on the first floor, overlooking the concourse, provided excellent meals at reasonable prices, and the Windsor Rooms were a stately, old-fashioned, typically English tea-room staffed by attentive waitresses in black-and-white uniforms. The Long Bar was a favourite resort of many tired businessmen returning home. All these establishments have long since disappeared, and today there is a large variety of fast-food outlets, as well as a 'French restaurant' situated, oddly enough, on the site of the former gentlemen's lavatory in the south station.

Below the passenger station, which stands high above the surrounding streets, there is a huge rabbit-warren of passages and stores, with at the lowest level the well-known 'Drain', the Waterloo & City Railway which was only the second 'tube' to be opened in London, just after the turn of the century. Its antique rolling stock is in process of replacement, and the passages and platforms have already been brightened. The only connection between the 'Drain' and the main lines above is by means of a lift, which enables carriages to be taken away and brought back when repairs are needed.

Waterloo (East) is a four-platform through station, unremarkable except for the decorative capitals of the cast-iron columns that support the platform awnings, and which have now been picked out in colour. There is no trace of the former junction and link with the main station.

Victoria Station

Victoria Station (or stations, since there are really two, connected only by an opening in a party wall) is today, as it has always been, something of a muddle. When Lady Bracknell was told in *The Importance of Being Earnest* that Mr Worthing had been found as a baby in 'a handbag at Victoria Station – the Brighton Line', she retorted, 'The line is immaterial.' For countless travellers, however, it has been essential to know whether their train departed from the 'Chatham side' or the 'Brighton side', something it was not always easy to ascertain, especially before the hole in the wall was cut, in those days when the two stations pretended to ignore each other's existence.

The Brighton side was the product of a major building scheme, starting in 1900 and completed in 1908. The frontage in 'Edwardian baroque' was the work of the London, Brighton & South Coast Railway's chief engineer, Sir Charles Morgan. It well matches the Grosvenor Hotel next door in its ornate, substantial, rather dull style.

The smaller twin station of the former London, Chatham & Dover Railway dates from 1862, so far as the arched train shed is concerned. For many years this was complemented only by wooden 'shacks', providing booking offices and similar passenger facilities, and a huge hoarding advertising the LCDR as serving 'Paris, Brussels, Cologne, Switzerland, Italy and [*sic*] India'. After the formation in 1899 of the South Eastern & Chatham Railway, merging the LCDR with its old rival the South Eastern for management purposes, the present office block and frontage were built, the architect being A.W. Blomfield. It is a 'Renaissance' effort in Portland stone, rather less ornate than the 'shop next door'. For many years the tradition of advertising the

Continental services on the frontage continued, with the slogan 'Sea Passage One Hour' – something that the shipping services fall short of achieving even today on the Dover-Calais service.

The Chatham side had many associations with the 1914-18 war, since the leave trains from and to the Western Front used its platforms, and ambulance trains brought back thousands of wounded, giving the station an eerie quality to anyone with a vivid sense of history.

In addition, it has always had close connections with royal occasions. Originally Victoria was used for special trains from Dover, where visiting sovereigns would land; but the most usual connection today is with Gatwick Airport. Platform 2 is particularly suitable for the reception of VIPs, being spacious and flanked by a suitably dignified waiting-room on the far side of which carriages can stand in the roadway, ready for either the direct drive to Buckingham Palace or a longer processional route through the West End. Pullman cars have normally been used for the relatively short journeys by these royal specials to Victoria, instead of the royal train used for longer journeys within Britain.

Victoria (Brighton side) occupies a long and narrow site bounded by the Chatham side to the east and Buckingham Palace Road to the west. So when the station had to be enlarged in 1908, it was lengthened rather than widened, giving some platforms a length of as much as 300 yards, enabling them to hold, if necessary, two trains, end to end. This feature has virtually disappeared with the enlargement of the concourse in recent years.

Victoria is still something of a muddle, despite some refurbishment. Matters have not been improved, except, perhaps, from the commercial standpoint, by the inclusion of the British Caledonian air terminal within the passenger concourse. However, major redevelopment proposals are progressing, including rafting over the railway tracks. There is also rebuilding of the old railway offices on the Chatham side – the offices where James Staats Forbes used to mastermind his long-drawn-out war with the South Eastern Railway headed by Sir Edward Watkin.

The Grosvenor Hotel was originally built by an independent company, in 1861, the architect being J.T. Knowles, in what is described as 'an Italianate style but with a French renaissance roof'. It was bought by the London, Brighton & South Coast Railway some thirty years later and leased to Gordon Hotels, one of the two main firms founded by Frederick Gordon – the other being Frederick Hotels, which for long provided catering on the London & South Western, and later the Southern Railway.

Victoria (Brighton side) Station, heavily masked by the Grosvenor Hotel and the forecourt bus station

When the station was largely rebuilt, in 1908, the hotel was also considerably enlarged. It has now been sold outright under the 'privatization' policy applied to British Rail's marketable assets.

Paddington Station

Paddington is the furthest from central London of all the main line termini. In fact, when this site was selected by the Great Western Railway (originally the London & Bristol Railway), it was only a second choice; the original idea had been to join the London & Birmingham Railway and share its terminus at Euston Grove. The lines are in fact little more than a stone's throw apart at Old Oak Common. However, the two Railway Boards were unable to agree on the terms for the use of Euston by the GWR; matters were further complicated when Brunel persuaded his Directors to adopt the broad gauge of 7 feet $0\frac{1}{4}$ inches for their railway instead of the London and Birmingham's use of the standard (4 feet $8\frac{1}{2}$ inches) gauge.

The Great Western line was thus diverted to a terminus at Paddington, then a village to the west of the Edgware Road. The site chosen was not that of the present station, but one even further out. It later became Paddington Goods Station and after that a large depot for National Carriers Ltd.

The present station dates from 1854 and was one of the last great works of Isambard Kingdom Brunel. J.B. Priestley considered St Pancras the most cathedral-like station, but Paddington must have an equal claim. As originally built, it comprises a 'nave', two 'aisles' and two 'transepts', the latter being a feature of particular interest. The unity of the concept was a little spoilt when a further bay or 'nave' on the north side was added in 1916.

When Paddington was built, Paxton's Crystal Palace was only a few years old. Brunel was one of the Victorian engineers who followed him in exploiting the possibilities of building great structures in wrought iron and glass. He employed an architect, Digby Wyatt, for the splendid decorative treatment which can still be enjoyed by the visitor – iron trellis-work on the ribs of the girders, mouldings and filigree work along the south wall, and end-screens at the Praed Street or buffer-stop end of the roof. The columns and balconies along Platform 1 display a 'Moorish' character, and there are oriel windows looking onto Eastbourne Terrace.

The plan of the station was originally the standard one for termini in the early days, a departure platform (now Platform 1) along which were strung the principal passenger requirements: booking office, waiting and refreshment rooms and of course station offices. Alongside the arrival platform (now No. 8) was a cab road for the convenience of arriving passengers. One consequence of this was a lack of any proper concourse or circulating area behind the buffer stops. For many years this space was used by Post Office and parcels vans, amid which passengers had to pick their way; it was known, incongruously, as 'the Lawn', the legend being that it was originally the garden of the stationmaster's house. However, in 1933 it was brought into use as a circulating area, and the parcels traffic was banished to another site.

A stroll along Platform 1 brings one to the wide footbridge which originally constituted the only convenient link between the departure and arrival sides, and it is important to look up to first-floor level to view the decorative features already mentioned. The entrance to the royal waiting-room, much used by Queen Victoria for journeys to and from Windsor, can also be identified on this platform.

The clerical offices that adjoin Platform 1, formerly the headquarters of the Great Western Railway, are dull on their street frontage, but they contain some fine early Victorian rooms originally designed for the GWR Chairman and Directors. Eastbourne Terrace,

Paddington without passengers! A wartime picture showing women porters

which they border, was occupied until rebuilding after the Second World War by a number of sleazy hotels, whose use was sometimes watched with ribald amusement by GWR staff working in the offices across the road.

There is a subsidiary office block adjacent to the GW Hotel on the Praed Street frontage; it was built in the 1930s for the Superintendent of the Line's department and is even duller than the older block along Eastbourne Terrace. But Brunel's and Digby Wyatt's work cannot be spoiled by these uninspired additions.

Paddington is essentially a main-line station – its 40,000 daily passengers are relatively few in comparison with Waterloo's 180,000. Suburban trains creep in and out infrequently, between the high-speed trains that occupy most of the platforms.

The whole train shed is a listed building, though the concourse has recently been enlarged by moving the buffer stops outwards, and new facilities, especially retail outlets, are being provided within the main structure, as well as a new booking hall.

The hotel was for many years popular with travellers to and from the West of England, offering them solid comfort rather than a smart modern ambience. It was originally designed by P.C. Hardwick, the architect of the Great Hall at Euston, in a French Renaissance style, including caryatids, balconies and a *porte-cochère* on the Praed Street frontage. Unfortunately, in the 1930s it was rather crudely refaced, as part of the station alterations then in process, and lost some of its former individual character, although then (and again since the war), extensive improvements in the facilities offered to guests were introduced. However, it has now been sold by British Rail – and in any case it never quite matched the station in the way that Gilbert Scott's St Pancras Hotel matched Barlow's train shed.

Marylebone

Of London's fourteen main-line termini, most are reasonably busy all day; four (Cannon Street, Holborn Viaduct, Blackfriars and Fenchurch Street) only justify their existence at busy periods during the morning and evening flows of daily commuters. But Marylebone is never a scene of real activity. It was designed to be a main-line terminus – the last to be opened in London, in 1899 – but it never fulfilled the hopes that led to its construction, and today it serves only two suburban lines, one reaching Aylesbury and the other High Wycombe, with a sparse service of trains continuing as far as Banbury. Marylebone in fact continues to earn the description given it by an eminent Catholic priest as the best place in London in which to meditate; an ornithologist has observed that no other station is so full of bird-song.

Sir Edward Watkin was the last of the great Victorian railway tycoons. He was a Manchester man, for long Chairman of the Manchester, Sheffield & Lincolnshire Railway, who collected railway directorships and chairmanships as other men collect pictures or racehorses. When, in addition to the MS&L, he was Chairman of the Metropolitan Railway, the South Eastern Railway and the Channel Tunnel Company, 'Manchester to Paris' became one of his dreams. He launched the building of Britain's last trunk main line, from Annesley in the Nottinghamshire coalfield south through Nottingham, Leicester and Rugby to join the Metropolitan Railway's extension line at Quainton Road, just north of Aylesbury. Ill-health forced him to retire in 1894, well before the line was opened in 1899, by which time the Manchester, Sheffield & Lincolnshire Railway had changed its name to Great Central.

Sadly, the GCR was never able to compete effectively with the older-established railways, even though its trains were fast (over a longer route), clean and comfortable, with particularly good dining and buffet cars. The London extension was a financial millstone round the neck of the Great Central, and Marylebone Station, with four platforms (but designed to accommodate eight in due course) was always under-utilized. Today the whole line from Annesley to

Marylebone Station; the frontage is listed and the station has been reprieved from closure

Quainton Road has been closed by BR, and Marylebone is left with only the commuter services mentioned. North of Aylesbury this once quite impressive trunk line, beautifully engineered, lies derelict, apart from activity by railway preservation societies at Quainton Road and at Loughborough.

It is therefore not surprising that BR long considered closing Marylebone and transferring the Aylesbury services to London Transport, whose trains already run as far as Amersham. Electrification onward to Aylesbury (barely fourteen miles) would be no problem. The services to the High Wycombe line could be transferred to Paddington. There were, however, strong protests from users of Marylebone and an increase in traffic over London Transport's line made it difficult, if not impossible, to transfer the Aylesbury services to Baker Street. Marylebone has therefore been indefinitely reprieved.

Since nationalization in 1948 (before which the station had belonged to the London & North Eastern Railway and had housed that company's board room and Secretary's office), uncertainty over its future led to curious changes. At first it came under the Eastern Region (all the station signs being re-lettered in that region's dark-blue livery); then transferred to the Western Region (all signs changed to chocolate and cream); and lastly to the London Midland Region (signs changed to maroon, the rather dismal version of the splendid Midland Railway's 'crimson lake').

But Marylebone has had its interesting moments. From here Winston Churchill left by special train one night for his historic meeting with President Roosevelt in mid-Atlantic. British Rail has often used it for exhibition purposes, showing new designs of rolling stock and testing public reaction. Film companies have frequently taken over its unused platforms; should Marylebone close, where would all those heartbreaking partings at railway stations be filmed?

Rejoicing at its reprieve need not obscure the fact that its architecture is not really very distinguished. The Great Central seems to have economized on architects' fees by having the design prepared in their chief engineer's drawing office. To quote George Dow, the historian of the Great Central Railway, Marylebone's walls are 'lined with Doulton terra-cotta ... the upper portion being faced with cream-coloured enamel bricks ... the facing was of "Redbank" pressed bricks, with dressings of Doulton buff terra-cotta'.

Across the carriageway from the station stands No. 222 Marylebone Road, formerly the chief headquarters office of the British Railways Board, the architect being Colonel R.W. Edis, who also built the Abercorn Rooms for the Great Eastern Hotel. It matches the station in its brick construction with terra-cotta facings, but it was not constructed by the railway. Sir Blundell Maple, a financier and friend of Sir Sam Fay, General Manager of the GCR, formed a syndicate to lease the site from the GCR and construct the hotel, which was then managed by Frederick Hotels. George Dow has written that the hotel's roof 'embodied a cycle track on which tycoons of the times could recover from gastronomic excesses or over-indulgence in other pleasures, notably among the choice *filles de joie* of nearby St John's Wood'.

After these rather raffish early days – including champagne parties for Sir Sam Fay, a considerable *bon viveur* – the hotel settled down to a more sedate life. Its publicity in 1903 claimed that it was 'designed to afford all the comfort and refinement of a well-ordered mansion without its attendant anxiety and also without extravagant outlay'. Sir John Betjeman has described how an orchestra playing in the Winter Garden and the stained-glass windows adorning the great staircase helped to make it popular both with travellers from the Midlands and with housewives from the commuter belt of the Chiltern Hills who, after shopping in London, had time for afternoon tea before their homeward train left from the station opposite.

Known as 'the Kremlin' to the railway staff who worked there after it was turned into offices in 1948, it was unsuitable for its new purpose but was nevertheless retained for thirty-eight years before being sold; the BR staff moved out only at the end of 1986. It looks forward to a new phase of life as an hotel once more.

Kensington Olympia Station

This station, though not architecturally important, is a significant part of London's railway history and was heavily used for nearly eighty years. The buildings are only a fragment of what formerly stood on the site, yet the wide spacing of the tracks suggests that they were originally laid to the 'mixed' gauge, (Brunel's 7 feet $0\frac{1}{4}$ inches for the Great Western plus standard 4 feet $8\frac{1}{2}$ inches), and the bay platforms as well as through platforms suggest its former importance. The previous station buildings, erected in the 1860s, were very 'London & North Western' in character, with saw-tooth platform awnings and substantial offices, including refreshment rooms and booking offices, on each side of the railway. Most were destroyed by bombing in 1940.

The station has had various names: 'Kensington', 'Addison Road', 'Kensington (Addison Road)', 'Olympia' and 'Kensington Olympia'. It is now the only intermediate station on the West London Line which links the Western and London Midland Regions with the Southern Region – a most important link, even though the freight traffic passing over it is only a fraction of what it used to be. But as late as the 1930s there were some 130 passenger trains working in and out of Addison Road (as it then was) every day. Electric trains ran to Edgware Road, Willesden Junction and Earls Court, steam trains to Clapham Junction. Even this density of traffic did not equal that in mid-Victorian days, when both 'Outer Circle' and 'Middle Circle' steam trains traversed the West London line, together with several other long-forgotten services, much patronized in the days when horse-cabs and horse-buses made cross-London journeys slow and tedious. Through trains between the Midlands and the south coast were appreciated by residents of Kensington who could thereby avoid the journey to a Central London terminus. The scanty remains of the original buildings are now supplemented by new facilities, since a number of through services from the North and Midlands to the south coast have been reintroduced by BR. The London Underground also operates a shuttle service from and to Earls Court.

The massive London and North Western Railway signal box at Olympia Station (operating Great Western type signals installed after nationalization!) testifies to the station's former importance

London Regional Transport

It might be thought that the London Underground system is too modern to offer much of historic interest, but the first section of the Underground, the world's pioneer in this field, was opened in 1863, from Paddington to Farringdon. Some of its early architecture remains and more has been imaginatively restored. Over and above this historical influence, there is the flowering of urban railway architecture, inaugurated by Frank Pick in the inter-war years, above all in the design of station buildings by his architect coadjutor, Charles Holden. So the mixture of the old and the relatively new makes a visit to selected sections of London's Underground rewarding. A major programme of renovation of stations, mainly on the deep-level 'tube' network, has been in progress for some time, and the results – not always ones that would have appealed to Pick or Holden – are frequently interesting.

Baker Street Station

At first sight, London Transport's Baker Street Station, crushed under the solid mass of the building named Chiltern Court, including flats and shops, seems to offer little of interest. However, it is really three stations. Platforms 1 to 4, just below street level, are the terminus of the former Metropolitan Railway's extension line, which started as a single-track offshoot of the Inner Circle as far as Swiss Cottage. Progressively widened and extended, it became the main route of the Metropolitan, which loved to describe itself as 'a trunk line in miniature'. Out into what it later called 'Metroland' (affectionately commemorated by Sir John Betjeman), it pushed in the 1880s and 1890s, finally joining the Great Central near Aylesbury in that railway's audacious drive southwards to London, and even extending a branch into a remote corner of the south Midlands at Verney Junction, between Oxford and Bletchley. Today these four platforms accommodate London Transport's electric trains to Watford, Uxbridge and Amersham.

Many Londoners can still remember when the extension line trains were hauled by locomotives – electric as far out as Rickmansworth (Harrow, until 1923), and steam thereafter. From 1910 until the outbreak of war in 1939 there were actually two Pullman cars (*Mayflower* and *Galatea*) in which one could ride in luxury, seated at a table with a pink-shaded lamp, on payment of a supplement above the first-class fare of 6d for travel to stations as far as Rickmansworth, or a shilling to stations further out. Theatre-goers travelling homewards on the midnight train from Baker Street could have a late supper in the Pullman, and breakfast was served to morning commuters.

These platforms were sometimes also visited by the two 'Rothschild' saloons, formed into a special train and used originally by the financier Ferdinand de Rothschild for his journeys between his palatial house near Wendover and London; and later for the Metropolitan Railway Directors' own special trains.

Platforms 5 and 6 on the Circle Line were the two original platforms when in 1863 the line was opened from Farringdon to Paddington. Their present interest lies mainly in the slanting shafts,

Charing Cross Underground Station murals by David Gentleman, illustrating the design and building of the original Eleanor Cross in the thirteenth century

lined with yellow brick, which originally helped disperse the smoke and steam before electrification and are now imaginatively restored, with hidden lighting. It is hard to imagine the nature of the atmosphere at 'Inner Circle' stations in those days: a very frequent train service was provided and, even though the engines were required to put their exhaust steam into their water tanks to condense it, this was not really effective and did nothing to remove the smoke. The sulphurous conditions on the Circle were a standing joke in Victorian times, though the railway issued statistics proving the longevity of its engine-drivers. This was derided by *Punch*, which asked why, in that case, the railway did not charge extra for this beneficial therapy!

Another section of Baker Street worth viewing is the Sherlock Holmes mural in the low-level 'tube' station; the Edwardian booking hall is also under restoration.

55 Broadway, Westminster

The former District Railway had its head office, architecturally undistinguished but adequate for its needs, adjacent to St James's Park Station. With the growth of the so-called London Traffic Combine, which involved the amalgamation of the District with three 'tube' railways to form the Underground Electric Railways of London, and the later inclusion of the London General Omnibus Company, office accommodation problems became acute.

The 'combine' was headed by Lord Ashfield as Chairman, with Frank Pick as Managing Director. Pick's interest in design and the visual arts was unique among transport leaders. Given financial authority to provide a new and fitting headquarters for the combine, Pick turned to Charles Holden for the design and the architect rose splendidly to the challenge. The difficult site allocated to him was an unbalanced rhomboid, partly straddling the railway tracks and the station platforms. Holden conceived a building of cruciform shape, with a central tower containing the lifts and services, and wings accommodating the offices, all of which enjoy external light. The disposition of the building's masses, faced with Portland stone, is dramatic; the only weakness is the lack of street space from which properly to view this building, now splendid with cleaned stonework.

Some architectural writers have described 55 Broadway as the most satisfactory building erected in Central London in modern times. It was unfortunate that its completion in 1930 led to an acute controversy, not about the merits of the building but about those of the two sculptures on the frontage, entitled 'Night' and 'Day' respectively, commissioned by the architect from the sculptor Jacob Epstein. Although they are only fifteen feet above pavement level, they are seldom noticed today, despite being well worth study. There are also eight sculptures, just above the sixth-floor windows and thus barely visible from below, which are by no means negligible, two being works by Eric Gill and Henry Moore.

The Dummy Houses

When the Metropolitan Railway – the world's first underground urban system – was extended westwards in 1866-8 from Paddington to Notting Hill Gate and Kensington, it passed under various select

Above: *The Dummy Houses in Leinster Gardens – favourite addresses for Victorian jokers to use*

Left: *Charles Holden's masterpiece: No 55 Broadway, built for the Underground group in 1929*

Victorian squares and terraces whose occupants raised vigorous objections to the arrival of the railway; the inhabitants of Leinster Gardens, which the railway crossed at a right-angle, were particularly vociferous. This delayed the work considerably and in the end the engineer, the redoubtable Sir John Fowler (1817-98), had to placate protesters by concealing the presence of the railway behind dummy façades exactly matching the adjacent houses on either side. Nos 23 and 24 Leinster Gardens became a favourite subject of Victorian practical jokers, who would not only order parcels or telegrams to be delivered there but would also summon the fire brigade or an undertaker to the ghost addresses.

Access: Queensway Underground Station (Central Line) gives access to the Bayswater Road, from which a turning north into Leinster Terrace leads into Leinster Gardens.

London Transport Museum, Covent Garden
Before the British Transport Commission was abolished in 1962, British Railways and London Transport shared the use of a museum in Clapham, South London. The BR exhibits eventually went to the National Railway Museum at York (a branch of the Science Museum); London Transport's exhibits, after a period at Syon Park, found a permanent home when Covent Garden fruit and vegetable market moved to Nine Elms. The splendid glass-roofed Victorian hall that had housed the flower market was taken over and provides a fine setting for a remarkable range of exhibits: the history of London's public transport is illustrated by a steam locomotive from the world's first underground railway, and by electric trains, trams and horse- and motor-buses, together with displays of posters, models and working exhibits such as signals and points that visitors can operate themselves.

Hatch End Station
The former London & North Western Railway, with its prestige express trains and its huge freight business, was not primarily interested in suburban traffic. However, it did everything in a big way, and some of its stations between the Euston terminus and Watford were not only spacious but architecturally interesting; several had clocktowers and a mixture of half-timbering and brickwork that was attractive.

Almost all have gone: Wembley is under a huge shopping complex on a raft above the railway; Watford Junction is now drowned within a new office block; Harrow is still associated with the terrible accident of 1952, when three main-line trains were involved in a collision with heavy loss of life.

'Steam-roller' locomotive that worked for years on the Wotton Tramway, and an early District Railway carriage in the London Transport Museum

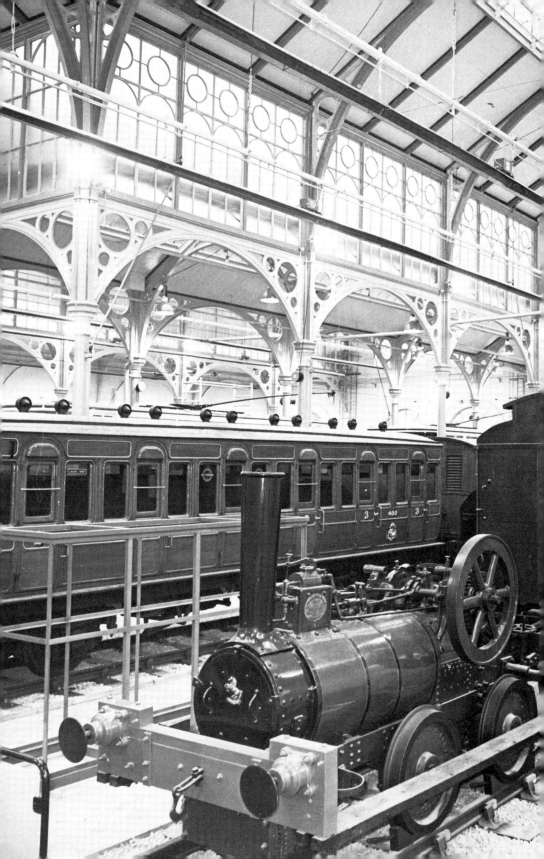

Hatch End Station: a good 'Queen Anne revival' building by G. Horsley

Greenwich Station, formerly run-down, has been well restored to its solid mid-Victorian dignity

One station, however, retains some of its LNWR character – Hatch End. When the 'new line' for suburban trains to Watford was built alongside the four main-line tracks in 1912, it was necessary to design and construct station buildings for the new pair of tracks. Most of these were uninteresting, but at Hatch End an attractive block was built on the down side which survives and is well worth a visit. The building may be described as 'Queen Anne revival' with slight Dutch overtones. Anyway, it is quite charming and blends in admirably with the suburban greenery of its surroundings.

Greenwich Station

The original London & Greenwich Railway was built on an almost continuous viaduct from London Bridge Station to a terminus just west of the present Greenwich station. In fact, if one stands on the up platform of the latter, one can see the end of the 1838 stretch, from which a sharp curve leads into the present station.

The original railway had quite a hard task to attract passengers away from the long-established river services to Greenwich round the Isle of Dogs. One promotional measure was to provide brass bands which played tunes as the trains left the two terminal stations! The London & Greenwich lost its individual character, however, when it was absorbed by the South Eastern Railway in 1845.

This is a good Victorian building, erected in 1878 by the South Eastern Railway. It replaces an older building, some of whose materials are said to be incorporated in the present rather grand structure, with its 'Tuscan' columns and elegant windows. The booking hall has a 'Grecian' character (a tiny echo of Euston's former Great Hall), and the building has recently undergone a cleaning that has revealed its qualities quite well.

Wharncliffe Viaduct

When Brunel was laying out the Great Western Railway from London to Bristol, the first engineering work of importance after leaving London was the viaduct at Hanwell, eight miles from Paddington, spanning the valley of the River Brent. Here he built a handsome structure 300 yards long and sixty-five feet high, with eight arches. The brick piers were interestingly shaped, being slightly conical, with stone capitals. On its completion, the Directors of the GWR named it after Lord Wharncliffe, who had been Chairman of the House of Lords Committee that had reported (favourably) on the Great Western Railway Bill to incorporate the company; his coat-of-arms was carved on the centre of the south face.

Although the viaduct has been doubled in width to accommodate four instead of the original two tracks, it remains an elegant structure, well worth inspecting.

Access: By road, leaving London in a westward direction by the A4020 (continuation of Oxford Street, Bayswater and Holland Park Avenue into Uxbridge Road), a good view can be obtained from the dual-carriageway section just beyond Hanwell. OS map 176.

Windmill Bridge, Southall

In 1855 the Great Western Railway promoted a branch from Southall, nine miles west of Paddington, to Brentford on the Thames, where the railway built its own dock to handle river traffic that had previously transferred to the Grand Junction Canal at that point. The branch was originally double-line and broad gauge, with both passenger- and freight-train services. Later one track was relaid as 'mixed' gauge for freight trains of both gauges, the passenger trains being all broad gauge. In 1875 the broad gauge was removed, and today the branch is only a single line, for freight exclusively.

In laying out the branch, it was necessary to cross a road named Windmill Lane, at a point where the Grand Junction Canal also crossed the road. Here Brunel designed a unique structure carrying

Brunel's first great work westwards from London on the way to Bristol: the Wharncliffe Viaduct (with his Lordship's coat of arms well displayed).

Brunel's ingenuity is well displayed at Windmill Bridge, Southall

the road over both rail and canal, putting the canal into an iron trough, over the railway but under the road. It is a curiosity of Victorian engineering, well worth a visit.

Access: By road, Windmill Lane is a turning south from the London–Uxbridge road (A4020) at the point where the Great Western main line crosses it between Hanwell and Southall by a massive bridge, itself worth inspection. Windmill Lane Bridge is about a third of a mile south of the intersection. OS map 176. (Windmill Bridge is only a short distance from Wharncliffe Viaduct which can conveniently be viewed on the same occasion.)

2. The Home Counties

Introduction

This section of the book covers a broad area of country around the metropolis – very roughly the 'commuter belt'. Commuting today, with the extension of motorways and railway electrification, has, however, become elastic – London workers commute not merely from Brighton and St Albans but from Winchester and Northampton, Colchester and Peterborough.

The chief obstacles to railway construction in the Home Counties were the Thames, the Chiltern Hills and the North Downs in Surrey and Kent. Major railway engineering works are not, however, very numerous. Among viaducts, Welwyn, Watford and Eynsford are important, as are Maidenhead Bridge and Brunel's two other bridges over the Thames between Reading and Didcot. The Chilterns are responsible for tunnels at Watford, Berkhamsted, Welwyn and Ponsbourne – all in Hertfordshire; the eastern end of the Chilterns, or 'East Anglian Heights', caused the short Audley End tunnels to be constructed on the Great Eastern Cambridge main line. The North Downs involved major tunnels at Sevenoaks, Polhill, Merstham, Oxted and Guildford.

Since this is so largely commuter-land, a great deal of station modernization has taken place, especially in connection with electrification. The majority of stations that have retained much of their original character are to be found, perhaps surprisingly, on the electrified Southern Region. This is partly because most of the Southern was electrified quite long ago, before the last war; partly because its General Manager, the great Sir Herbert Walker, insisted that electrification and station reconstruction were separate projects. If stations required rebuilding, the expenditure must be justified separately and not be included as part of the electrification package. That may account for the survival of some attractive stations such as Boxhill and Westhumble, virtually untouched from early steam days though now on a busy, electrified route – a bonus for everyone with

A Victorian Royal party leaving Windsor Central Station, as reconstructed on site by Madame Tussaud's

an eye for a good railway building. Where the Southern *did* rebuild, however, one may have mixed feelings. Stations in concrete, such as Richmond, are in a style that could be described as 'Southern Odeon' – advanced for its 1930s period, but now looking rather dated, yet scarcely 'historic'. Other Southern Railway stations, such as Woking, were rebuilt in a no-nonsense brick idiom.

The Great Western tended to do everything in the grand manner, with wide platforms and substantial buildings all along the main line, but designed by engineers rather than architects. It took the proximity of royalty to persuade the GWR to look beyond mere efficiency and become decorative, as at Windsor. (The London & South Western had challenged it in the royal borough, already.) Here and there a GWR survival from a much earlier period can be found, as at Mortimer. On the North Western side, most individual station characteristics have disappeared under electrification and modernization. The Midland main line formerly had a charming station at Mill Hill with characteristic saw-tooth glass platform canopies – long since swept away.

The Great Northern main line out of King's Cross was always unremarkable for stations. The GNR had grudged spending on them,

though it had to build a fine viaduct and numerous tunnels. The Great
Eastern also lacked stations of any distinction until the line from
London had stretched far into East Anglia. South of the Thames, the
perpetually warring South Eastern and London, Chatham & Dover
Railways had little cash for stations of distinction. The London,
Brighton & South Coast was the most eccentric in this field, in some
cases splashing out money on lavish station buildings, in others
grudging its passengers much more than a wooden shack! It was
tunnels and viaducts that really distinguished the LBSCR. The London
& South Western also, apart from Windsor as described below,
bequeathed little of architectural interest to the Southern Railway in
the Home Counties. By and large, therefore, the railway archaeologist
needs to travel beyond commuter-land for the most rewarding sites.
Even so, nearly a score are listed here as well deserving a visit.

Windsor Stations

'Royal Windsor' was first served by the Great Western Railway,
which reached it in 1849 – but only two months before the London &
South Western Railway arrived from another direction. The GWR
had tried to enter Windsor as long ago as 1834 but the implacable
opposition of Eton College forced it to withdraw an application for
Parliamentary powers. Fifteen years later, the branch from Slough
was constructed but subject to strict conditions imposed by the
College. It was, however, built to Brunel's seven-foot broad gauge and
was therefore not very convenient for Queen Victoria, who used royal
trains for many journeys – above all for her regular stays at Balmoral
and Osborne on the Isle of Wight. Accordingly, if the royal saloon had
to be worked from other railways' lines to Windsor, the LSWR's
Riverside Station had to be used – hence that railway's description of
itself as a 'Royal Road'. Queen Victoria had in fact given permission in
1848 for the LSWR to cross the Home Park of Windsor Castle so as
to reach the town, and by so doing had done herself a favour.

However, in 1862 narrow-gauge rails were laid between Slough &
Windsor (GWR) Station, and thereafter many royal journeys were
made from and to that station, where a sumptuous royal
waiting-room was eventually built in 1897. The Windsor branch
trains ran into Slough Station facing towards London, but a junction
was put in for the opposite direction which was mainly needed for
royal journeys, and hence was always known as 'the Queen's Curve'.

Today the station is totally out of scale with the train service – a
shuttle diesel to and from Slough – since it includes a wide cab road
with an elliptical glazed roof, an ornamental office block and, adjacent
to the royal waiting-room, a roofed-over area large enough for

The famous flattened arch, so daringly built by Brunel, frames a lovely riverside picture at Maidenhead

processions or military escorts to form up. Funeral trains for Queen Victoria, King Edward VII, King George V and King George VI have all been accommodated at Windsor Central, with the cortèges to the castle starting from the station.

In 1983 a permanent exhibition was opened in the station by Madame Tussaud's on the theme of 'Royalty and Railways', including a re-creation of the arrival of a royal train conveying Queen Victoria.

Windsor & Eton Riverside Station was designed by Sir William Tite, who built many charming stations for the LSWR. Rather sadly, it lost much of its importance for Queen Victoria's journeys after 1862, though it has been used in recent years for royal trains on the Southern Region. It is well suited for ceremonial occasions, having its own royal waiting-room separate from the main building. Both buildings are architecturally interesting: the style is predominantly Tudor in red brick and includes a lofty booking hall with an oriel window and a bell turret; the brickwork facing Datchet Road is particularly intricate and repays study.

Maidenhead Bridge

After the Wharncliffe Viaduct, the next important structure on Brunel's London to Bristol railway was the Maidenhead Bridge over the River Thames (which is actually nearer to Taplow than to Maidenhead). To effect the crossing, Brunel designed a brick bridge with two arches of half-elliptical shape, flatter and larger than any

Mortimer Station is an original Brunel timber station with verandah roof, well deserving its restoration

built up to that date. The result was a most graceful and pleasing design that can still be admired today.

Brunel encountered fierce criticism for designing such flat arches, which were considered unsafe, and for a time the critics were delighted to observe a slight subsidence in the eastern arch in the spring of 1938. Brunel identified this as a failure on the part of the contractor, due to easing the timber centring before the cement had set properly, and this was quickly rectified. To appease his critics, however, he agreed to leave the timber centring in place until the spring of 1840. There were congratulations when the centring was blown down in a storm in the autumn of 1839 but the arches stood firm. What Brunel did not reveal was that the centring had been eased in the previous spring, so that the arch had stood unsupported for six months – as it has ever since.

Access: There is a view from the A4 London–Maidenhead road, stopping about one mile to the east of the centre of Maidenhead. OS map 175.

Mortimer Station

This station, between Reading and Basingstoke, shares with Charlbury the distinction of being one of the few survivors of Brunel's standard timber stations with verandah roofs. It has been carefully restored to its original condition, including replacement of the slated roof by pantiles.

Great Western Railway 'Pagodas'

At the beginning of this century, the Great Western Railway decided to stimulate local and short-distance traffic in several areas by providing a more frequent train service with 'auto-trains' which usually consisted of a locomotive and one or two open carriages operating on a push-and-pull system. At the same time, a number of simple unstaffed 'halts' were opened; these featured a standard form of shelter with a corrugated-metal construction and a highly individual curved roof with an Oriental flavour. These were promptly nicknamed 'pagodas' and were to be found at many places on the GWR system. Many have now disappeared though examples can be seen at South Greenford Halt and at Appleford Halt near Didcot.

The Great Western Railway erected some 'halts' with curious corrugated-iron platform shelters known to the staff as 'pagodas'. These are at Appleford Halt near Didcot

Wolverton Viaduct and Works

Freeling's *Guide to the London & Birmingham Railway*, published to coincide with the opening of the line in 1838, began with the words 'This is a ROMAN work', and it is true that the Romans, who built stupendous aqueducts (a pity they had not understood the principle of the siphon), would probably have classed Robert Stephenson's Wolverton Viaduct, to the north of Wolverton Station on the main line out of Euston, as ranking with some of their own major works. It is not very long (220 yards) but is a beautifully balanced structure with elliptical brick arches of sixty-eight-foot span, narrow side arches at each end, and a fine stone cornice.

Wolverton was an important railway centre for many years. As a half-way point between London and Birmingham, formerly all trains stopped here. There was a famous refreshment room, described in Sir Francis Head's *Stokers and Pokers* as staffed by 'seven very young ladies to wait upon the passengers', presided over by a 'Matron or Generalissima'. The morals of the 'very young ladies' had to be exceptional; Head wrote that, 'the breath of slander has never ventured to sully the reputations of these paragons', of whom four 'have managed to make excellent marriages'.

Apart from the passenger station and the creature comforts it offered, Wolverton was for many years also a forerunner of Crewe and Derby. Locomotives were built here until 1862, and carriage-building for the London & North Western, London Midland & Scottish and British Railways, including several royal trains, had a long and distinguished subsequent history. Travellers today notice only a slight reduction in speed as the trains take the sweeping curve that was put in when the main line was diverted around the site of the works (it formerly ran through their centre on a straight alignment). Soon after comes the 1½-mile-long embankment over the valley of the Northamptonshire Ouse, in whose centre is the Wolverton Viaduct.

Access: By train, only quick views of the Works and viaduct are possible. By road, the viaduct can be viewed from a side turning north, off the A5, leaving the roundabout at the north end of Milton Keynes. OS map 152.

Fenny Stratford Station

For many years 'Oxbridge' academics complained about the lack of a fast train service between the two ancient universities despite the fact that the same railway – originally the London & North Western and afterwards the London Midland & Scottish – served both cities by branches from its main line at Bletchley. Moreover these were laid out so that through-running was possible., But the agricultural nature of the country through which these two lines passed – Bedford being the

Wolverton Viaduct's beautifully balanced and elliptical arches have a classic elegance

principal town *en route* – discouraged the running of anything but stopping trains of a leisurely character. This led to a good many jokes at college high tables about arranging inter-University conferences in Bletchley Station waiting-room.

The LMS Railway was not insensitive to these complaints and in 1938 made an interesting experiment with a pioneer three-car diesel multiple-unit set which ran between Oxford and Cambridge.

Today the section from Cambridge to Bletchley is completely closed. The line from Bletchley to Bedford is all that remains of the Oxford–Cambridge line.

About a mile from Bletchley Station is situated Fenny Stratford Station, on the old A1 Watling Street road, away from the railway junction of Bletchley and the huge encroachment of the new town of Milton Keynes. Built in 1846, it is a completely charming building in a Tudoresque rustic style – half-timbered with dormer windows, gables and fretted bargeboards. The reason for this style was the alleged wish to match buildings on the Duke of Bedford's estate at Woburn, where many such cottages for estate workers existed. The style was described by earlier writers as *cottage orné* and by 1876 might have seemed a throwback to the romantic movement satirized

Fenny Stratford: half-timbered and totally Tudoresque

in Thomas Love Peacock's novels *Headlong Hall* and *Nightmare Abbey*. Woburn Sands Station, three miles away, is almost an identical period piece.

Southill Station (closed)
In the 1840s the Midland Railway grew tired of handing over its growing London traffic to the London & North Western Railway at Rugby, especially in view of the delays caused by congestion between

Rugby and London. In 1853 powers were obtained for a line from Leicester to Bedford and thence to Hitchin on the Great Northern Railway, which gave the Midland a second route for its traffic to London and one with a much greater length over its own metals and thus more remunerative. The railway was opened in 1857; however, after little more than ten years, dissatisfaction with the Great Northern's handling of Midland Railway traffic led the latter company to build its own line from Bedford to London direct.

This meant that the section from Bedford to Hitchin had constituted a major main line for only about a decade before it was bypassed and reduced to branch-line status. However, it contained three intermediate passenger stations of great charm, all in the same architectural idiom: Southill, Shefford and Henlow.

The line has long been closed, but Southill Station survives as a private house in that delightful village. It is in characteristic 'Midland cottage-Gothic' style.

Access: The A600 Bedford–Hitchin road crosses the A507 Milton Keynes–Letchworth road in the village of Shefford. From it, a mile north of Shefford, a side road is signposted to Southill. From London, the roundabout on the A1(M) north of Baldock gives access to the A507 for Shefford and Southill. OS map 153.

Southill: part of a former station used as a private house

Welwyn Viaduct

The Great Northern Railway did not believe in spending money on ornament, so the Welwyn Viaduct, spanning the valley of the Mimram River $21\frac{1}{2}$ miles north of King's Cross Station, was as severe in its plain brickwork as that terminus itself. Yet it is a fine and satisfactory structure, even if it lacks the special character of Rastrick's Ouse Viaduct or Brunel's Wharncliffe Viaduct. It has no fewer than forty arches, at a maximum height of a hundred feet over the valley.

The GNR was haunted by a (quite unfounded) fear that the viaduct might give trouble; this was one reason for extending the Hertford North branch to rejoin the main line near Stevenage, thus providing a diversionary loopline route should it be needed. It has often proved useful. Legend has it that in a dense fog one day a goods train halted in the neighbourhood. The guard alighted at what he took to be Welwyn North Station platform and walked up and down, stamping his feet to warm them. Suddenly the fog lifted for a few seconds and he discovered that he had been prancing about on the parapet of the viaduct!

Access: By train, although the view of the Mimram valley from above is charming, one cannot appreciate the viaduct's character. By road, leave the A1(M) at the roundabout signposted for Tewin and Hertford for a minor road passing below the viaduct. OS map 166.

Audley End Station

The Northern & Eastern Railway was born as a proposed railway from London to York via Cambridge, but it obtained Parliamentary powers in 1836 only to go as far as Cambridge; shortage of money, in fact, meant that it took four years to cover even the $15\frac{1}{4}$ miles to Broxbourne, and two more years to reach Bishops Stortford. Another spasm of construction took it as far as Newport (Essex), sixteen miles short of Cambridge; then, exhausted, it handed itself over to the Eastern Counties Railway, which injected new life into the project and got the line built as far as Cambridge and Ely by midsummer 1845.

In that year a particularly attractive station was built at Wendens Ambo, a village about half-way between Bishop's Stortford and Cambridge, the architect of the station being Francis Thompson. The local grandee, through whose land the railway passed here, was Lord Braybrooke of Audley End House. Care was taken to follow standards approved by his lordship, in addition to changing the name of the station from Wenden to Audley End.

It is a charming building, which has been well restored in recent years by BR's Eastern Region. The main building is well balanced, a two-storey block between single-storey wings, with verandahs and pleasant round-headed windows. At the road entrance there is a fine *porte-cochère* where Lord Braybrooke's visitors using the railway could avoid contact with the weather outside.

Audley End Station

Elsenham Station

Anyone who wishes to sample the flavour of the 'country railway', in a typical countryside, can hardly do better than take one of the London to Cambridge slow trains that call at Elsenham, between Bishops Stortford and Cambridge. It retains the authentic atmosphere of the former Great Eastern Railway: the two platforms are staggered – an arrangement often favoured because the expense of a footbridge could be avoided thereby.

The up platform contains timber buildings, with a heavy projecting awning supported on cast-iron columns that have decorative features. It is a small, practical, 'engineer's structure', very characteristic of the company that built it.

Formerly a delightful single-line branch wandered from here across country to the unspoilt medieval town of Thaxted, with its magnificent church. Today it is difficult to imagine Elsenham Station as a junction of significance.

The charm of the rural Great Eastern! Elsenham Station (up side) just before electrification of the line

Hertford East Station

The Northern & Eastern Railway threw out a branch to Ware and Hertford from its main line at Broxbourne just about the time it was being taken over by the Eastern Counties Railway in 1843. The two Hertfordshire towns thus gained a rather roundabout route to London via the Lea Valley and Stratford, though Hertford later obtained additional access to London via the Great Northern Railway.

Hertford East Station was rebuilt in 1888 by the Great Eastern Railway (as the Eastern Counties had become), the architect being W.N. Ashbee. It is characteristic of that railway's favoured manner: the so-called 'free renaissance' architectural style, in red brick with a massive *porte-cochère* somewhat out of scale for this station. The detail includes Jacobean gables, latticed stone parapets, carefully designed doors and windows, with a decorated ceiling in the booking hall. The whole effect is characteristic of the best sort of eclecticism that can be found in Victorian architecture and is well worth viewing.

Incidentally, Ware Station, two miles nearer London, although lacking the architectural interest of Hertford, is something of a curiosity. It is a single-platform station on a double-track line, reduced to single track through the station, the constriction arising from the proximity of the River Lea and the main road. Two trains (obviously) cannot be in the station at the same time, though Ware is a by no means inconsiderable town.

Gravesend Station
The South Eastern Railway, having taken over the working of the London & Greenwich Railway in 1845, extended the line along the south bank of the Thames. Eventually Dartford and Gravesend were reached by more than one route.

On the way towards the Medway towns, Gravesend was the most important place, and here the South Eastern built an attractive station in 1849. The architect, Samuel Beazley, provided a balanced building of classical elegance with a colonnade in the centre, flanked by two-storeyed blocks on either side, in yellow stock bricks with stucco dressings. The station, a Grade II listed building, was fully renovated by BR in 1978 and is well worth inspecting.

Gravesend Station, by Samuel Beazley, is a fine classical structure that has been well restored by BR

Eynsford Viaduct

Large and interesting viaducts are not very common near London. The Southern Region has many miles of low viaduct carrying its lines just above street and rooftop level, but few that cross river valleys – which are in any case mostly shallow around London – in spectacular fashion. An exception is the Eynsford Viaduct, built in 1862 by the Sevenoaks Railway, a little concern which in 1859 had obtained powers to build a line from Sutton-at-Hone (now Swanley) on the London, Chatham & Dover Railway (until that year named the East Kent Railway) to Sevenoaks, with a later extension to Maidstone. The Sevenoaks Railway was absorbed by the LC&DR in 1879.

Eynsford Viaduct crosses the valley of the River Darenth by nine arches, supported by elegant and slender brick piers; its distinctive appearance is enhanced by a pierced stone parapet of unusual design.

Access: By road, take the A225 Dartford–Sevenoaks road (Lillingstone Castle and a Roman villa are signposted near the viaduct.) OS map 188.

Aylesford Station

The South Eastern Railway, which covered the county of Kent, had a rather cavalier attitude towards the county town of Maidstone. Originally it merely sprouted a branch from its main line, $4\frac{1}{2}$ miles east of Tonbridge, to Maidstone in 1844, the junction station (now Paddock Wood) being then called Maidstone Road.

A second approach to the county town was completed in 1856, from Strood at the mouth of the Medway River. This was a projection of the North Kent line which, opened in 1847, utilized the tunnels through the chalk hills east of Gravesend, $2\frac{1}{2}$ miles long, originally built by the Thames and Medway Canal. That canal had been completed only in 1824; twenty-two years later it was bought up by the SER, drained and used for the extension of the railway to Strood.

This line via Strood still offered no more than a rather roundabout route to the county town, following the Medway valley. But on the way to Maidstone, several charming wayside stations were built, the best probably being Aylesford. It is in a sort of railway 'cottage-Tudor' style in Kentish ragstone, ornamented by stone quoins and slightly incongruous brick 'Tudor' chimneys.

Boxhill & Westhumble Station

The Vale of Mickleham, through which the River Mole flows from Dorking to Leatherhead, is one of the most beautiful areas in the Home Counties. The London, Brighton & South Coast Railway's line through this delightful valley included a station at the foot of Box

Aylesford Station is a splendid piece of railway 'cottage-Tudor'

Hill, which does not violate the surroundings. The land on which it stands could be acquired from a local landowner only on condition that the station must be of an ornamental character. The railway's architect, C.H. Driver, accepted the demand and produced a design with a markedly French character, including a turret with an ornamental and very Gallic crest of ironwork, steep gables and an entrance hall with a small hammerbeam roof. The effect is charming.

Leatherhead Station

For a considerable time the London & South Western and the London, Brighton & South Coast Railways were at loggerheads, especially over the Portsmouth traffic, culminating in the 1858 'Battle of Havant' (see p.73). Later, however, the two companies arranged matters more amicably and joined forces for a joint line between Epsom and Leatherhead, beyond which point the LSWR diverged to Effingham Junction and the LBSCR continued to Dorking.

But co-operation did not extend to joint stations; at Epsom for many years an LBSCR station was in use just east of the junction with

Boxhill and Westhumble: a splendid little piece of fantasy by C.H. Driver, not far from London

the LSWR and the latter's station was built to serve a pair of outside tracks only, the LBSCR lines passing between them. And at Leatherhead, two separate stations were constructed in 1867 though in sequence, on the same length of track. The LSWR station was a cheaply built affair, not very convenient for the town centre; the LBSCR one was much more impressive. C. Hamilton Ellis has written: 'When the South Western station was functioning separately over the way, the Brighton building seemed to be parading its undoubted superiority to, and absolute dissociation from, the seedy establishment adjoining.'

The Southern Railway ended this nonsense in 1927, closing and demolishing the former LSWR station and concentrating traffic on the ex-LBSCR station. This interesting building (architect C.H. Driver) has a French-looking turret and an elaborate façade with round-headed windows. The ironwork of the supporting columns for the awnings on the platforms and the frontage is delicate and worth study, as are the foliated capitals of the brick shafts between the windows.

At Leatherhead the ex-LBSCR station is much more substantial than the LSWR one was and survives today; a faint French influence can be detected

Godalming Station

The Portsmouth Direct Railway, which linked the London & South Western Railway near its former Godalming terminus with the London, Brighton & South Coast line at Havant, was a speculative venture which never owned any locomotives or rolling stock. It was built with the idea of selling itself to the London & South Western Railway but the negotiations hung fire, and for a time it tried to attract the South Eastern Railway by providing a connection, the earthworks for which can still be seen just south of Guildford. The South Eastern, however, declined, and eventually the LSWR, a much more appropriate purchaser, took it over and began to work trains over it. This led to the famous 'Battle of Havant' of 1858, when the LBSCR blocked the junction at that station, tore up the rails and attacked LSWR men endeavouring to force a way through with an engine, on the grounds that the LBSCR would experience 'unfair' competition for the London–Portsmouth traffic.

Although the line was built with cheapness as a main consideration, some pleasant station buildings were provided, the architect reputedly

Godalming is the best of the wayside stations on the Portsmouth Direct line, built in stone instead of brick

being Sir William Tite. Most were in brick; but Godalming was built of local rubble stone with ashlar facings of a most agreeable golden-brown texture. It is also more elaborate than its neighbours in possessing Tudor-style windows and a steep gable.

Recently the Friary Brewery, which had moved its headquarters to Godalming, offered to contribute towards the cost of a station 'face-lift'; the result has been most pleasing and is well worth inspection.

3. The South of England

Introduction

The tract of mostly beautiful country that lies between London and the English Channel was formerly served by three railways which sometimes competed and sometimes co-ordinated their activities. Each had a strong individuality, until they were welded together in the Southern Railway in 1923. It was usually possible, just by looking at a station or a signalbox, to decide whether the trains would be those of the London & South Western, the London, Brighton & South Coast or the South Eastern & Chatham. Of the three, the 'Brighton' was the most inclined to spend money on stations, and it had a number of handsome and spacious structures – remarkably, for a rather small railway. The 'South Western' had some fairly deplorable stations, even at important junctions such as Woking, until these were rebuilt by the Southern Railway after amalgamation; economy seemed to have been all-important to the LSWR. Much of the same attitude could be found on the 'South Eastern'. But it must be said that here and there on all three systems some reasonably good modern architecture could be found, for instance in the rebuilt Waterloo of the LSWR, and Dover Marine of the SECR, now renamed Dover (Western Docks).

Between the termini there was an enormous variety of smaller stations, including some with much charm and character – above all on the LBSCR. That railway also had three notable tunnels on its main line that pierced respectively the North Downs, the Forest Ridge and the South Downs, as well as spanning the Ouse valley with a splendid viaduct. The South Eastern also had some noteworthy tunnels, including three through the White Cliffs of Dover in the waterside stretch of line from Folkestone to Dover, together with the very impressive Foord Viaduct that carries the tracks high above the rooftops of Folkestone. By contrast the LSWR was rather short of impressive engineering works.

It was extraordinary that the little Isle of Wight formerly supported

– if that be the word, in view of their chronic impecuniosity – three railway companies: the Isle of Wight Railway, the Isle of Wight Central Railway and the Freshwater, Yarmouth & Newport Railway. Only the rump of the first-named now survives, electrified and operated by ex-Central Line tube trains. Old and rough-riding they certainly are, but they have preserved a tradition of railway service that would otherwise have perished. One steam-train preservation society has kept a short stretch of track open but elsewhere in the island traces of the old railways are hard to locate.

St Denys Station (Southampton)

Portsmouth, as mentioned previously, considered itself ill-used by the railway by comparison with Southampton, until the Direct Portsmouth Line was opened in 1858. It even lacked a good link with the rival port, a journey to or from which entailed a reversal at Bishopstoke (now Eastleigh), until 1866 when a more direct (if very curvaceous) line was opened from a northern suburb of Southampton at Portswood to Fareham and Portsmouth.

The station at Portswood was then renamed St Denys. It is quite an impressive affair, with platforms on both the main (London) line and Portsmouth line. It has a considerable affinity with the Italianate style of Sir William Tite's other stations for the original London and Southampton Railway built a quarter of a century earlier. It is brick with stone dressing and attractive fenestration, and a platform canopy quite well integrated with the main building.

Gosport Station (closed)

Portsmouth's traditional rivalry with Southampton was aggravated when in 1841 the London & Southampton Railway considered it sufficient to serve the great naval base by merely building a short branch to Gosport, on the opposite side of Portsmouth harbour, which entailed ferrying Portsmouth passengers across the harbour. Some of the grievance was removed when a line was built into Portsmouth itself, though by quite a roundabout route, which served until the Direct Line was built in 1858. Meanwhile it was as a sop to Portsmouth that the railway's name was changed to London & South Western.

Whether or not the idea was partly to mollify Portsmouth, the railway company built a very fine station at Gosport. It was opened in 1841, the architect being Sir William Tite. It was in pure classical style, with a long colonnade in Portland stone. At each end there are pavilions, again in pure classical or Tuscan style.

When Queen Victoria travelled to and from Osborne House on the

Sir William Tite's grand Italianate station at St Denys

Isle of Wight, she used the Gosport route, but the royal yacht sailed to and from Clarence Navy Yard and, after a time, a short railway was built, with a private station for the Queen's use, into the yard.

The branch line and Gosport Station are now closed: the station was badly damaged in a fire, but even in its ruined state it is spectacular. A visitor might be excused for thinking that it was formerly some Greek or Roman temple. It is well worth inspection.

Access: The Gosport bus station and the adjacent Portsmouth ferry terminal are opposite a roundabout, from which Mumby Road leads off on a curving course ending at a junction with Spring Gardens Lane, opposite which stands the former station. OS map 196.

Wareham Station

When the London & Southampton Railway, having transformed itself into the London & South Western, began seeking to expand westwards from Southampton, its first objective was not just Bournemouth but Wareham and Dorchester, with the idea of continuing – despite fierce opposition from the Great Western – towards Exeter. However, the eventual terminus of this line became Weymouth, reached as the result of an amicable settlement of the Exeter project by obtaining 'running powers' over the Great Western's Yeovil to Weymouth line.

No rivalry arose, however, over the branch from Wareham to Swanage, which was opened in 1885. To serve the junction, a handsome station was built in 1886; it is now a listed building, Grade

Wareham: a mixture of Flemish, Queen Anne, and Norman Shaw-type architecture

II, and officially described as 'in the Flemish– Queen Anne style inspired by the work of Norman Shaw and J.J. Stevenson'. It has fine gables, and decorative stone panels showing the railway coat-of-arms, and a cupola with a weather-vane.

Ouse Viaduct

Between London and Brighton, as well as the three great tunnels, there is another notable engineering work: the Ouse Viaduct between Balcombe and Haywards Heath. Anyone who thinks that one railway viaduct is very much like another will be surprised at the individuality – indeed, the beauty – of this structure. It is only moderately lofty (ninety-two feet) as it crosses the shallow valley through which the infant Ouse runs, but its brickwork is outstanding, and special features include the oval openings in the piers, often photographed end-on, and the delightful little pavilions on both sides of the railway at the end of the thirty-seven arches which make up this elegant structure.

The viaduct was designed by the London & Brighton Railway's engineer, J. Urpeth Rastrick, in 1840; it has been suggested that the 'Italianate' pavilions were the work of the architect who built Brighton Station for the same railway, David Mocatta.

One of the classical early railway engineering triumphs: J.U. Rastrick's Ouse Viaduct

Access: By road, coming south, leave the M23 London–Brighton motorway at Junction 10 to join the B2036 for Balcombe; in Balcombe village, fork left for Haywards Heath (unclassified road), bringing one in a couple of miles close to the viaduct. Coming north, take the road from Haywards Heath signposted for Balcombe and Crawley. OS map 187.

Brighton Station

The London & Brighton Railway, which first linked the metropolis with the seaside in 1841, was fortunate in both its engineer, J.U. Rastrick, and its architect, David Mocatta, by whom the Brighton terminus was given a fine stucco building entirely in harmony with the Regency terraces of the town. It has an arcade of nine arches and a terrace above with a parapet: on either side are other arcades with columns. The first-floor windows, fifteen in all, have handsome pediments, alternately triangular and segmental. The central, curved, false gable bears a clock.

If Brighton Corporation had shown the same enlightenment as many Continental authorities, the station could have become the focal point of a grand highway leading down to the sea, like a French *place de la gare* or German *Hauptbahnhofsplatz*. But a typical British muddle of buildings of little worth has spoilt Mocatta's frontage – and the

Brighton was once proud of its terminus by David Mocatta, engraved soon after opening in 1841

railway rather compounded the offence in 1882 by erecting the glazed canopy in front of the arcade, useful but inelegant.

Behind Mocatta's building there is a fine train shed built much later in 1883 by H.E. Wallis, engineer of the London, Brighton & South Coast Railway. It is an ingeniously curved structure, coping admirably with the complex lay-out of tracks which diverge sharply within the station area on each side of the main line to London, to serve the 'West Coast' and 'East Coast' branches.

Clayton Tunnel

J.U. Rastrick's splendidly engineered London to Brighton Railway had three ranges of hills to traverse, in each case through tunnels of considerable length: at Merstham (North Downs), Balcombe (Forest Ridge) and Clayton (South Downs). The Clayton Tunnel is interesting from a meterological point of view: many generations of travellers have noticed how often the weather changes where the train emerges, a dull day to the north turning to bright sunshine as Brighton is approached, south of the tunnel, or a sea-mist to the south becoming clear weather in the Sussex Weald on the other side of the Downs.

The tunnel mouth is a fine piece of castellated Victoriana. Between the twin towers stands, oddly enough, a cottage.

Access: None by rail. By car, from the A23(T) London–Brighton road, turn sharply north for Clayton village (view of tunnel), three-quarters of a mile south of Pyecombe and about six miles north of Brighton. From the east, Clayton is reached from Ditchling via the B2112. OS map 198.

Foord Viaduct, Folkestone

The original London–Dover route of the South Eastern Railway, opened in 1844, was built in virtually a straight line across country from Redhill to Ashford, parallel with the line of the North Downs and with no gradients of any consequence. Beyond Ashford, the line curved south to approach the coast; then at Folkestone came the first major obstacle faced by the engineer, Sir William Cubitt, the 'Foord Gap', in which the upper part of that town lies. This he crossed by a high-level brick viaduct a hundred feet high, with nineteen arches, looking down on the roofs of the town. The view from a train passing over it is spectacular, extending over the harbour to the Channel.

Battle Station

Every schoolchild knows that the Battle of 'Hastings' took place in 1066. The year may be undisputed but the site was not Hastings but near the present village of Battle, some seven miles inland. Duke

Bestriding the upper part of the town of Folkestone, the Foord Viaduct is a spectacular work

William of Normandy swore that, if victorious, he would found an abbey, and in due course he did so in fulfilment of his oath. He could not have foreseen that the ecclesiastical architecture of Battle Abbey would eventually influence the design of a railway station!

Battle village enjoys a picturesque station on the Tunbridge Wells to Hastings line, built by the former South Eastern Railway and opened in 1852. The railway had been extended from Tonbridge (then usually spelt Tunbridge) to Tunbridge Wells as early as 1845. The competing Brighton Railway's line reached St Leonards in 1846 and Hastings – by a short length of SER metals – in 1852.

Today Battle Station, whose architect was William Tress, is as good a medieval replica as one could desire: it has a central hall with cross wings; there are splendid lancet windows in the waiting-room; there is even a belfry.

Etchingham Station
Etchingham, eight miles north of Battle on the Tunbridge Wells–Hastings line, is interesting in its 'Tudor' style, differing from

One of the finest castellated entrances, with a cottage snugly hiding behind its parapet, is Clayton Tunnel through the South Downs

Etchingham is a fine essay in the Tudor manner by the South Eastern Railway

both the medieval/ecclesiastical manner adopted by its architect, William Tress, at Battle, and his 'Italianate' manner at St Leonards (Warrior Square). The railway company seems to have given him a very free hand!

Etchingham is extremely attractive, using stone in two contrasting shades. Historians have suggested that it may also have had the distinction of being in 1858 the first place to be served by a 'slip carriage' detached from a non-stopping train.

It must be said that this charming station in the heart of rural Kent has seen better days, as regards the trains serving it. Today's modernized but still rather austere electric trains are a considerable improvement on the post-war diesel trains known to Southern railwaymen as 'paraffin cans'; but they are still a far cry from the South Eastern Railway's 'Hastings American Car Train' of the 1890s which offered a form of luxury travel unusual for that period, or the six Pullman cars that the Southern Railway introduced on the Hastings service in 1926. Those latter trains moreover were later often hauled by the splendid 'Schools' class of locomotive which over this hilly route performed wonderfully as well as looking glamorous.

Dover: (Western Docks) Station

This is today a rather sad place, but worth a visit by those with a sense of railway history. After the South Eastern and the London, Chatham & Dover Railways formed a working union in 1899, their new Managing Committee decided to straighten out the tangle of railways in Dover, and especially to improve conditions for cross-Channel passengers. Between them, the two rivals had built stations at Dover Town and Dover Harbour (SER) and Dover Priory (LCDR); they shared (not always amicably) the use of Dover Pier Station, alongside which their ships berthed. To replace the Pier Station, a fine four-platform terminus was built by the SECR with an all-over roof and an imposing stone-faced portal where the tracks enter. It was virtually complete in 1914, but of course for the four years of war was used mainly for Services traffic. After the war ended, the station was brought into full use; for long it accommodated the *Golden Arrow*, as well as less glamorous boat trains. Its use changed during the Second World War yet again.

After the war ended, Dover took up once more its role as a major passenger port station; but the progressive shift towards the roll-on, roll-off road business, and away from the 'classic' rail-sea passenger traffic, coupled with the opening of the vast new complex at Dover's Eastern Docks, led to a decline in the use of Dover Marine, signalized by its being rechristened 'Western Docks'. Now it has only a fraction of its former importance, though a few ferry ships still use the Western Docks, as does the jet-foil service to Ostend. But the Pullman cars – indeed all refreshment cars – have, sadly, vanished from the ordinary electric trains that now alone connect with the marine services.

It is worth noting that from the sea-wall beside the station, extending along the breakwater, a fine view can be obtained of the busy shipping traffic in the harbour.

The impressive portal to Dover Western Docks looks like a real gateway to the Continent

Devotees of E.F. Benson's Miss Mapp *books will recognize Rye Station as that of 'Tilling' in the novels. It was one of the South Eastern Railway's better efforts*

Rye Station

'Ancient Rye', as the house-agents love to call it, with its fascinating collection of noteworthy houses clustered round the splendid church on the top of the hill, is not let down by its station, built by the South Eastern Railway in 1851, architect William Tress. It stands at the foot of the hill, and somehow its faintly Renaissance or 'Italianate' character does not clash with the glorious mixture of medieval and eighteenth-century houses that adorn the streets of this celebrated town, the 'Tilling' of E.F. Benson's charming *Miss Mapp* novels.

The station building is symmetrical, with a front of five bays, the three central ones constituting an entrance loggia. Even the platform side is quite attractive, not being disfigured by the later canopy.

4. The Midlands and East Anglia

Introduction
The west Midlands are not merely the traditional home of the motor industry but also possess the most car-minded population in Britain. Yet there remains a dense network of railway lines serving the region, formerly belonging to three great companies, the London & North Western, the Great Western and the Midland. Now all are included within British Rail's London Midland Region, with headquarters in Birmingham, the railway crossroads where the main line from London to the North-West and Scotland crosses the trunk line between the North-East and the South-West. From New Street Station trains seem to leave for all points of the compass.

New Street, modernized in the 1960s, is today a convenient station, but essentially a utilitarian one, sunk beneath a huge shopping complex and therefore lacking any architectural interest in its own right. It is in complete contrast with the classic façade of historic but abandoned Curzon Street, marooned among buildings that have nothing to do with the modern railway, still seeming to dream of the time when the early steam trains from London terminated there.

Snow Hill was the Great Western's chief station in central Birmingham; it is presently being rebuilt. The purpose of disused viaducts like the one at Duddesden is difficult to identify except from old railway maps, and the cat's cradle of railway lines in and around 'Brum' is matched only by the fantastic network of canals within the city limits. The west Midlands are a territory in which the railways were conspicuously preceded by the canal age and succeeded by the motor age. Perhaps a future generation may regard the Gravelly Hill motorway interchange ('Spaghetti Junction') much as we today look at Duddesden Viaduct.

The Potteries show some curious contrasts in railway structures. The North Staffordshire Railway had a notable station at Stoke-on-Trent, the capital of the Potteries, and some attractive stations elsewhere. Others were very different. Arnold Bennett, in one of his stories of the Five Towns, wrote: 'The train stopped at an incredible station situated in the centre of a rolling desert whose surface consisted of broken pots and cinders.' In fact, it was Burslem, on the former loop line of the North Stafford.

In complete contrast is the highly picturesque entrance to Shugborough Tunnel on the Trent Valley line of the former London & North Western, often photographed. And further north, in Cheshire, the Weaver Viaduct is noteworthy. As well as Chester Station itself, the rail approach through the city wall is remarkable.

The scenery of the north Midlands is more dramatic than that of the west Midlands; both regions were, however, cradles of the Industrial Revolution. Derbyshire is significant for both industrial and railway sites. Richard Arkwright's original textile mill at Cromford is a landmark of industrial archaeology, as are the remains of the Cromford & High Peak Railway for railway historians.

Sadly, the splendid scenic route of the Midland Railway through the Peak District from Derby to Manchester has been cut back at Matlock. But scenery and archaeology combine to make the whole area inteesting. And fortunately the Midland's Sheffield-Manchester line, which crosses the Peak District from east to west, as the Derby-Manchester line formerly did from south to north, is still open. Its most scenic stretch is in the Hope Valley, between the two great tunnels of Totley and Cowburn.

Derby was the heart and the head of the Midland Railway, whose former general offices still stretch alongside the partly modernized station. The BR Technical Centre now dominates the London Road exit from the town and is a good example of modern functional architecture.

On the east side of the county, the former Midland main line passes close to George Stephenson's retirement home at Tapton, near Chesterfield, close to the industrialism of Clay Cross. At Butterley (whence came the ironwork for St Pancras Station's roof) the Midland Railway Society preserves many interesting relics of that highly individual railway company.

The east Midlands were competitive territory. The Great Northern, the Midland, the Great Central, the Great Eastern and even the London & North Western jostled one another in the search for traffic, sometimes duplicating routes and stations, sometimes joining forces against a third party. A pre-grouping Railway Clearing House map shows a bewildering mixture of colours denoting basic company ownership, with bi-coloured lines showing joint ownership.

Of the railways concerned, the Midland was perhaps the most inclined to spend money on its stations, Leicester and Nottingham being typical of its larger structures. Less typical but more charming was Market Harborough Station, shared by the Midland and the LNWR and quite recently restored. Lincoln was fortunate in having two stations, each of which has merit. St Mark's has been the subject of careful restoration. However, the geography of the area – for the most part gently undulating – has not produced many striking engineering structures: bridges over waterways, rather than tunnels under hills, being characteristic. One splendid viaduct, at Harringworth, deserves a visit, and several railway byways repay exploration. The site of the abandoned Nottingham Victoria Station, once an important railway centre, reveals a major victim of the Beeching axe. It joins Edinburgh's Princes Street, Manchester's Central and Glasgow's St Enoch as an example of vanished grandeur.

As some compensation, a closed station at Sandon, between Colwich and Stoke-on-Trent, has been sold to a buyer who intends to restore its attractive 'Jacobean' architecture; Atherstone, between Nuneaton and Tamworth, is another case of restoration.

The huge bulge of land, bordered by the North Sea, that comprises East Anglia was served for over a century by, virtually, a single railway, first called the Eastern Counties then, from 1862, the Great Eastern. True, at the southern extremity there was the little London, Tilbury & Southend Railway, and across northern Norfolk, the Midland & Great Northern Joint Railway traversed the Great Eastern main lines with a route linking the Midlands with Norwich, Cromer, Yarmouth and Lowestoft. Nevertheless, on the map the GER was almost everywhere predominant. Its two main routes from London both ran to Norwich, one via Colchester and Ipswich and the other via Cambridge and Ely; in between, and on either side of the main lines, a complex network of branches served this mainly agricultural area.

Perhaps for that reason the Great Eastern was always known to railwaymen as 'The Swedey'. Although never very prosperous, it was surprisingly efficient in many ways. It coped with a huge London suburban traffic, with Continental services based on Harwich and with a lot of miscellaneous freight. The architecture of its stations near London was unimpressive, but out in the country there were some good buildings, such as those at Norwich, Bury St Edmunds and Felixstowe. Proximity to the North Sea may have been responsible for a faint Dutch character in some façades.

The popular idea (outside East Anglia) that it is a level region ('Very flat, Norfolk,' was a famous Noël Coward character's sole comment) is erroneous. Most of the terrain traversed by the former GER is undulating, though only modestly so. However, the railway was built cheaply; it was never flush of money and so it has many

Curzon Street's Ionic columns echo the Doric of the vanished Euston Arch

quite steep, if short, gradients to avoid the need for expensive earthworks and structures. East Anglia therefore has relatively few impressive railway viaducts or picturesque tunnels. It is the station buildings, including some on closed branch lines, that are most worth visiting.

Birmingham (Curzon Street) Station

J.C. Bourne's well-known series of drawings of the London & Birmingham Railway opened with Philip Hardwick's stark Doric arch or 'Propylaeum' at the London end and finished with the graceful Ionic columns of the same architect's Birmingham terminus at Curzon Street. Considering that in the same year, 1833, in which the London & Birmingham secured its Act of Parliament, the Grand Junction Railway also had obtained powers for its route from Birmingham to join the Liverpool & Manchester Railway, it was odd that a terminus rather than a through station should have been laid out, in Birmingham, by Robert Stephenson for the L&B Railway. A joint through station might have seemed an obvious piece of collaboration. However, for some seventeen years – in fact, until well after the amalgamation of the two companies had taken place in 1846 – there were separate, though adjacent, terminal stations for the two railways, which made through working difficult, and inconvenient for passengers.

Osborne's *Guide to the Grand Junction Railway* of 1838 was in no doubt that the L&B station, opened in that year, was the finer of the two. It was splendid, 'consisting of a massive and magnificent building for offices, a handsome line of booking offices, two beautiful and gigantic sheds ... and the engine house, a circular building with a prodigiously strong floor'.

These two stations were soon joined by a third nearby, the terminus of the Birmingham & Derby Railway in Lawley Street, which crossed Curzon Street. This complex quickly established Birmingham as a major railway centre.

Osborne certainly did his best to promote rail travel from Birmingham by his enthusiastic descriptions of scenes at the station: 'Two or three plans for the formation of a new street from the Stations to the centre of the town, have been proposed .... This will offer an inducement, and excite a desire for travelling, which at present do not and cannot exist.' Quite far-sightedly, too, Osborne called for the provision at the station of 'something that is not at present publicly projected that we know of, yet is felt to be generally needed – a Railroad Tavern'.

Pending these desirable improvements, Osborne vividly described the scene on the departure platform:

Porters with ladders are mounting and placing luggage on the tops, passengers are taking their seats, and arranging themselves for the journey; young ladies, who have been, or who are going on a visit, accompanied by their mammas on one side, and lovers on the other, the servant man or maid following with band-box, are saluted and tended until they are safely packed in their places, and all the paraphernalia of veil, boa, cloak, muff, and reticule containing biscuits and oranges, scent bottle and purse, with change ready for use – are properly ordered. Old travellers, who have been most of their lives on stage coaches, take their places, and being accustomed to prepare at a moment's notice, seat themselves, and quietly look on.

Anon come some young gentlemen, whose lips are employed to smoke cigars, and let a few syllables drop by accident! Dressed as if for the saloon of a theatre, and bestowing a few glances of admiration on the affair, as short as their observation and superficial as their understanding, they exclaim with a peculiar mark of sagacity, 'Very fine, by Jove!' 'Just the thing egad', or 'Know how to do the thing, damme.'

There is an echo of stage-coach days in the advice to the intelligent traveller:

If you wish to see and hear all about the matter, take your place outside. You will want an extra great coat, and a pair of gauze spectacles to keep the dust and smoke out of your eyes; but, in all other respects, you will enjoy ten times more than your fellow travellers.

Moving over to the arrival side, Osborne is equally lyrical.

The carriage glide ... so smoothly and quietly, that they seem to be self-moving; and the order and regularity, the dignity and importance of the train, give the whole matter an air of national grandeur. Every train seems a royal cortège; every passenger a person of distinction.

These charming scenes in Curzon Street and nearby ended when in 1854 the much-needed Birmingham through station was opened at New Street; Curzon Street, with its neighbour, was turned over to goods traffic. The 'magnificent' office building became the goods department offices, and the whole complex suffered by adaptation to purposes for which it had never been designed. The classical exterior, however, remains in essentials and is well worth visiting.

Access: In central Birmingham. Curzon Street leads east from the inner ring road (one-way system).

Chester Road Station

Rather improbably, a charmingly rustic, wooden ex-London & North Western Railway station house is to be found at Chester Road, on the Lichfield–Redditch commuter route which runs through the congested central area of Birmingham. It is just six miles from New Street Station and enjoys a frequent diesel train service, funded by the West Midlands Passenger Transport Executive. The station looks as if

Chester Road Station is charmingly rural, though only six miles from the heart of Birmingham

it should be on some Oxfordshire country branch line: its arched windows and overhanging roof in lieu of a platform awning give it a distinctive character.

Stoke-on-Trent Station

Stoke, the capital of the Potteries, was re-christened 'Knype' by Arnold Bennett in his 'Five Towns' novels. The North Staffordshire Railway (known as 'the Knotty' after the county badge, the Staffordshire Knot) had its headquarters offices here. Local patriotism was strong and, whatever the criticisms of the train service, 'the Knotty' was strong on stations. At Stoke, the station was built in 1848 in a Jacobean style, with much ornamentation allegedly copied from an historic original. The building also housed the board room and headquarters offices of the NSR – hence its grandeur.

Facing the station is Winton Square, planned by the railway and dominated by the North Stafford Hotel (1849) which in its architecture admirably complements the station. The remainder of the square is occupied by houses also built by the railway's architect. In the centre of the square stands a bronze statue of Josiah Wedgwood, so that the whole composition forms a most impressive gateway to the Potteries.

Stone Station

This station is a few miles south of Stoke-on-Trent on the main line of the former North Staffordshire Railway. It is the junction where the two connections from the NSR to the ex-London & North Western main line (one via Stafford, one direct to Colwich) part company. The

Stone Station: perhaps the best of all the 'Knotty's' lesser Jacobean efforts

station house stands in the angle of the junction and is one of the best examples of 'North Stafford Jacobean' with its three large gables, each topped by a spike, repeated back and front of the building. It is quite dramatic and well worth a visit.

Shugborough Park Tunnel

The Trent Valley Railway was promoted in 1845 from Rugby to Stafford, avoiding Birmingham and shortening the route from London to Liverpool and Manchester. The principal engineer was Robert Stephenson, but he was associated with G.P. Bidder, his lifelong friend and later a President of the Institution of Civil

This fantastic, castellated entrance to Shugborough Park Tunnel was demanded by the Earl of Lichfield

Engineers. At Colwich the railway was laid out to cross Shugborough Park, the seat of the Earl of Lichfield. In consideration of the Earl's agreement to sell the land and not to oppose the company's Bill in the House of Lords, the Trent Valley Railway Company agreed to provide an ornamented bridge for the line, in classical style, across one of the drives through the park. The result is something like an eighteenth-century 'folly', a bridge with Ionic columns, curved wing walls (with balustrades) and a parapet with plinths on which are displayed the Lichfield arms, with a lion and a seahorse as supporters! Unfortunately, the rail traveller cannot appreciate this bridge as he rushes over it at speed.

In addition, the tunnel (774 yards) in the park had to have fantastically decorative entrance portals. The line here is running more or less east and west; the eastern portal (the down-side entrance) is in what has been described as an Egyptian style, still embodying the Lichfield arms. But the western (up) portal is yet more exotic. BR describes it as being 'in Norman style, with battlements, gargoyle-like corbels, and a pair of turrets decorated with crenellations'.

Access: By train, scarcely a glimpse can be obtained from the window: trains are usually travelling too fast here. By road, apply to the National Trust, which now owns Shugborough Hall – which incidentally houses the Staffordshire County Museum and so is doubly worth a visit. The A513 leads south from Stafford to the park. OS maps 127 and 128.

Charlbury Station

Built in 1853 by the Oxford, Worcester & Wolverhampton Railway, this little station is worth visiting because it has been carefully restored to its original condition. It was designed by Brunel, who was the engineer to the OWWR, appointed at a time when that railway was financially aided by the Great Western, of whose system its route was a natural extension. But it had a history of acrimonious disputes with its parent and was chronically short of money until it was finally absorbed in the West Midland Railway in 1860, which in turn became part of the GWR in 1863.

One consequence of the OW&WR (the 'Old Worse and Worse'), being short of funds was its need to build stations as cheaply as possible. Brunel accordingly provided at Charlbury a timber structure with a verandah projection from a hipped roof – simple, effective and rather charming.

Stivichall (Coventry): Coat of Arms Bridge

If one is motoring between Coventry and Leamington on the A444, (OS map 140), it is worth stopping just before the railway bridge at

Brunel could build cheaply but still attractively, as at Charlbury

Stivichall and pulling off the road (practicable) for a minute or two to admire the handsome bridge built in 1844 for the London & Birmingham Railway's branch to Leamington.

Not only is the elliptical arch in the local red sandstone very handsome but in the centre there is a large stone displaying the arms of the local lords of the manor, the Gregories of Stivichall – a nice feudal touch that would not have appealed to the great Dr Arnold, Headmaster of Rugby, who, watching a train on the L&BR said, 'I rejoice to see it, and to think that feudality has gone for ever.'

Cromford Station

Cromford is a name familiar to every student of economic history as one of the cradles of the Industrial Revolution in Britain. It was here that Richard Arkwright built his cotton-spinning frame operated by water-power, thus laying the foundations of the Manchester cotton trade. Arkwright was not the sole pioneer; he built on foundations laid by James Hargreaves and his 'spinning jenny', and was followed by Richard Crompton who developed the 'mule'; but Cromford is always remembered as the place where factory work and power machinery first revolutionized cotton spinning. It was said that Manchester men, while travelling by the Midland Railway, should have raised their hats or at least bowed their heads when passing Cromford Station!

Quite apart from this historical association, Cromford Station is well worth notice, even though it is no longer situated on the main line to Manchester, but merely on a branch from Derby, ending at Matlock. Its special feature is a waiting-room with an extraordinary, sharply pitched roof, with a turret over the door in a steeple form. The diamond-latticed windows are a typically cosy, 'cottagy' Midland Railway touch, but the turret and, behind it, the large stationmaster's house, are all oddly French in character, with delicate ironwork. The date is around 1860, and the architect was probably G.H. Stokes, an assistant to Sir Joseph Paxton whose influence (on behalf of the Duke of Devonshire at Chatsworth) seems to have spread over quite a stretch of the Midland's Derby–Manchester route ('the Manchester Bank' as the enginemen used to call it in the days of steam because of the long and severe gradients on either side of Peak Forest, up which they had to pound with the fireman working very hard to keep up boiler pressure).

Wingfield Station (closed)

Although George Hudson, the 'Railway King', was eventually convicted of cutting corners and even of endangering safety on his railways through economies designed to make the dividends appear more attractive, the railways he brought together to form the Midland Railway in 1844 were well engineered and equipped. In particular, the North Midland Railway from Derby to Leeds was graced by a series of charming stations in classical style by the architect Francis Thompson. Wingfield (1840) is a pavilion with flanking wings, in a dark ashlar stone that blends especially well with the Derbyshire countryside. A happy touch is the station name in carved gilt lettering surrounding an ornamental clock.

Access: The station has been closed and the building is in private ownership. A glimpse can be obtained from trains between Derby and Chesterfield; by road, take the B5035, turning west off the B6013 (Clay Cross to Heage road), signposted South Wingfield. OS maps 120 and 128.

Buxton Station

The Midland Railway's route from the south into Manchester through the splendid scenery of Derbyshire was built in stages, reaching Buxton by a branch in 1863, at the same time as the London & North Western reached it from Manchester. The Midland's enterprise aroused the anger of John Ruskin, who demanded to be told why a fool in Bakewell should be assisted to become a fool in Buxton within minutes. This early environmental outburst reads oddly today, when so many lament the closing of the Midland's splendidly engineered line through this picturesque and mountainous countryside.

Overleaf: *Cromford Station is extraordinarily French in its architecture – odd in the heart of Derbyshire*

The huge fanlight in the end wall of Buxton Station – still impressive despite demolition of most of the train shed

If Ruskin was not appeased, the same could not be said of the Duke of Devonshire, who, though imposing strict conditions about the preservation of amenities and the location of stations, agreed not to oppose the railway's construction. The Duke owned a large part of Buxton and was concerned that the town's appearance should be preserved in all ways. His interests were looked after by his agent and former head gardener at Chatsworth, Sir Joseph Paxton.

The Midland and LNWR stations were built side by side and appeared almost as twin structures from the street, having identical gabled ends with huge fan windows, edged with the railway company's name in gold lettering. Sadly, the Midland Station has now been demolished, with the closure of the line from Derby; but the LNWR station is still there and merits a visit.

Monsal Dale Viaduct
One of the most regretted casualties of the Beeching and

post-Beeching era has been the former Midland Railway scenic route between Derby and Manchester, north of Matlock. Not only did it pass through an area of dramatic scenic quality – as dramatic in its way as the Settle & Carlisle Line of the same system – but it contained a series of engineering works of importance, with tunnels and viaducts succeeding one another all the way from Ambergate to Chinley. Perhaps there is a slight compensation in the fact that today they can be viewed in leisurely fashion, where road access is adequate.

The Victorians christened this 'the Flute Line' because so much of it is in tunnel, often with only short open-air sections in between. These, however, especially in the High Peak area, were quite often on viaducts or bridges; one of the most notable was Monsal Dale Viaduct, built in 1863 by the Midland Railway's engineer, William Barlow. It is a listed building, no longer in BR ownership but in the hands of a railway preservation society.

Crossing the River Wye immediately after a tunnel is the spectacular Monsal Dale Viaduct

Its five arches cross what Ruskin, who was one of the earliest conservationists to appreciate the grandeur of the Derbyshire landscape, called 'the Vale of Tempe'. Nearly everyone today would agree that – unlike motorway interchanges – this railway structure both blends with and even enhances the splendid local scenery.

Access: None by train, of course – unless and until the preservation society achieves its aim of running trains between Buxton and Matlock. By road, take A6 Matlock to Buxton road along the Wye Valley. OS map1 119.

Nottingham Stations
Nottingham was formerly served by three main-line railways – the Midland, the Great Central and the Great Northern. The first two had imposing stations in the city; in addition, there were a number of suburban stations. Nottingham Victoria, the impressive but always under-utilized GCR and GNR joint station, has sunk (almost) without trace; London Road Low-Level and High-Level Stations are both closed, and the latter has been demolished. Nottingham Midland, however, survives: it dates only from the era of competition with the Great Central (then extending south to London), at the turn of the century. It is a good example of the Midland Railway's solidity and confidence, with its central clocktower and massive screen wall alongside London Road, all in terracotta and sandstone – broadly classical in emphasis, certainly lacking the Gothic influence felt so strongly in many Midland stations from St Pancras downwards. The glazed tiles and lantern of the large booking hall are a *fin-de-siècle* touch.

Stamford Stations
'Burghley House by Stamford Town', the ancestral home of the Cecil family, long dominated not merely the town of Stamford, $1\frac{1}{2}$ miles from its great park, but also the early railway promoters when they invaded this corner of England. The first arrival at Stamford was the Syston & Peterborough Railway, later absorbed by the Midland; it commissioned the architect Sancton Wood to design a station worthy not only of the great house nearby but also of the splendid domestic architecture of unspoiled Stamford. This he did with great success, providing a stone Tudor manor house as a station building, well preserved today by BR.

Less than a decade later, the Great Northern Railway, opened in 1850 to reach London from Yorkshire, sought its own link with Stamford. A small Stamford & Essendine Railway (later absorbed by the GNR) was built to connect the GNR main line at Essendine, a wayside station between Peterborough and Grantham, with Stamford

Nottingham Station: a typical important 'Midland' station façade

Stamford Station is not unworthy of the architecture of this almost unspoilt townscape

in 1856. The terminal of this branch was Stamford East; not to be outdone by the earlier arrival in the town, the station was designed by William Hurst in a Tudor style that proved quite acceptable to its neighbour in Burghley House, the Marquess of Exeter, who was also the chief shareholder in the Stamford & Essendine Railway. Since the closure of the Essendine branch, it has, however, been sold; it is no longer possible to view the large and impressive former booking hall, with its delicate balustraded gallery and lantern roof, or the offices of the little Stamford & Essendine Railway Company included in the station.

Kettering Station
The Midland Railway had many strong devotees, as is exemplified by the toy-makers of Nuremberg who early in the twentieth century seem to have exported to Britain more railway models in MR colours than in the livery of any other railway company. Certainly the Midland was distinctive in almost everything it did, not least in station design. A surviving Midland station can still be recognized at a glance, provided it has not been modified or insensitively enlarged by some district engineer. And of all the present-day survivors, Kettering is perhaps the best example of the famous Midland glazed awnings on cast-iron pillars, a ridge-and-furrow design with hipped ends – light, elegant and first-rate for its purpose. This design can also be studied in a fine example at Loughborough Station, twelve miles north of Leicester on the main line to Nottingham and Derby from London.

Kettering's station building, attributed to Charles Trubshaw and dating from 1890, is in brick and terra-cotta, with fine gables and ornamental chimneys. The island platform's awnings are older than the rest, dating from 1857, before the line was quadrupled; their ironwork differs from that on the main platform.

Harringworth Viaduct
In the days when Midland expresses from London to Nottingham used the direct route from Kettering via Oakham, passing over the Harringworth Viaduct was quite an experience: one wondered how much longer one was going to look down on the wide expanse of the Welland valley. The red-brick viaduct, built in 1879, is in fact 1,275 yards long, with no fewer than eighty-two arches, the longest on British Rail. Any monotony in the design was reduced by enlarging and decorating every sixth pier. It is very impressive.

During the Second World War, a number of aerial bombing attacks on the viaduct were made: the Germans evidently considered this line of railway – never as important as the original Midland main line via

Splendid ironwork on the platform canopies at Kettering

Leicester – to be a key transport link. None of the bombs put the viaduct out of commission.

Further along this line (now closed to passengers) is the section formerly used as a test track for the prototype Advanced Passenger Train which ran up and down at high speed for many months, testing its tilting mechanism with apparent success.

Access: None by rail. By car, take the A6003 linking Melton Mowbray with Kettering, turning east on to B672, two miles north of Rockingham, for an excellent view. OS map 129.

Market Harborough Station

Market Harborough, in the heart of fox-hunting country, is today known additionally for the canal-boat rallies that have been held there. But it is also a railway centre of some importance, though less than formerly. The London & North Western Railway built a station here when it constructed its branch from Northampton to Peterborough in 1844–5. When the Midland Railway later pushed south from Leicester to Bedford and Hitchin, in 1857, with the object of sending trains to London over the Great Northern Railway, it had to cross the LNWR at Market Harborough on the level – something that led to delays and recriminations. With the opening of the London extension of the MR in 1867, Market Harborough called for reconstruction, and agreement was reached with the LNWR for a flyover bridge coupled with station reconstruction. A new joint station

Harringworth Viaduct seems to stretch into infinity

for the two companies was completed in 1885.

The architecture of the new station building was a modern version of the 'Queen Anne' style, entirely charming. Red brick and stone pilasters, mouldings around doors and windows, and fine chimneystacks are all beautifully balanced. Restored, after some years of neglect, by BR in 1977-8, the building received an award and much favourable publicity in the architectural Press.

Wolferton former Royal Station and Museum

The railway line from King's Lynn to Hunstanton in Norfolk was opened in 1862 to develop the latter village as a seaside resort. Almost at once the small station at Wolferton, six miles from Lynn, became important when the Prince of Wales, later King Edward VII, purchased the large adjacent Sandringham estate.

Royal trains began to use the station so frequently that in 1898, when the line was doubled, the Great Eastern Railway (not without some hesitation over the expense) commissioned its architect, W.N. Ashbee, to provide a truly sumptuous new station at Wolferton for royal arrivals and departures. This was done in style. The resulting

building has a stone-and timber-framed exterior with 'Gothic Revival' details: a mixture of the cosy and the impressive. The interior, however, is the most important aspect, with the main hall and the two royal waiting-rooms (one used by King Edward VII and the other by Queen Alexandra for receiving guests). All has been lovingly restored, and many exhibits associated with royal journeys are on view, having been assembled from various sources; figures dressed in period costume add to the illusion.

The royal station handled no fewer than 645 royal trains between 1884 and 1911 – that period when King Edward VII was most frequently at Sandringham.

Having this close association with Sandringham, the local tradespeople had many anecdotes to tell of the royal family. One concerned the local clockmaker, who was awakened at five in the morning after the night when King George V died, with an urgent summons to Sandringham. There he received instructions to put back by half an hour every clock in Sandringham House and in every building on the estate. The reason lay in history. Edward VII had had a particular distaste for unpunctuality. (In fact, when Queen Victoria's

The former Royal Waiting Room beautifully restored at Wolferton

funeral train from Gosport to London started a few minutes late, the new King's reputation in this respect led to a record run being made to make up time, with some breakneck speeds of which the Queen would certainly *not* have approved.) He carried his hatred of unpunctuality so far as to order all clocks to be kept thirty minutes fast; and George V carried on this tradition at Sandringham. The Prince of Wales, however, did not see eye to eye with his father and grandfather in this, as in various other respects; when he became King Edward VIII, in 1936, he lost no time in restoring Greenwich time throughout his properties.

A peculiarity of royal journeys between Wolferton and London was that for many years use of the Great Eastern Railway terminus in London, Liverpool Street Station, was avoided, because the Sovereign would thereby have to enter the City of London and, by ancient custom, this involved the presence of the Lord Mayor and an exchange of formalities, including the offer and return of the City's Sword. The need for this ceremony was obviated by routing royal trains into and out of the Midland Railway terminus at St Pancras, when the Great Eastern Railway had running powers into that station; and later – after the 1923 grouping which amalgamated the Great Eastern with the Great Northern – into King's Cross, which is also outside the City boundary.

As King's Lynn is a terminus, royal trains had to reverse there, and the process of attaching another engine for the short run of six miles to Wolferton was time-consuming. After the advent of the motor car, it was usually more convenient for the royal passengers to alight from or join the train at King's Lynn and drive direct to or from Sandringham. This led to some disuse of the ornate accommodation at Wolferton. Still later, with the reduction in traffic and the growth of road competition, the line to Hunstanton closed in 1969; royal trains had already ceased to use the branch. The station was sold and now comprises a private dwelling plus the museum housing the exhibits mentioned above. It is open daily, April to September, on weekdays 11 a.m. to 1 p.m., and 2 to 6 p.m.; on Sundays 2 to 6 p.m. A small admission charge is made.

Access: A side road from the A149 Lynn to Hunstanton road leads west to Wolferton, the turning being just north of Babingley. OS map 132.

Market Harborough Station: a prize-winning example of good restoration work

A distinct Dutch character in the station buildings at Downham Market

Downham Market Station

Connoisseurs of the Fenland country that lies north of Cambridge, with its rather 'Dutch' character and splendid sky panoramas, will already know the architecture to be found in King's Lynn, as well as the majesty of Ely Cathedral rising on its little 'island' above the flats. But elsewhere domestic architecture is less interesting, and travelling by train between Cambridge and King's Lynn can be somewhat monotonous, partly on account of the reduced speed limits which the nature of the subsoil demands; this frustrates the fast running which the almost straight alignment would otherwise permit.

It is therefore pleasant to encounter a charming little station building (listed, Grade II) at Downham Market between Ely and Lynn, dating from 1848 and built for the Lynn & Ely Railway which was absorbed by the Eastern Counties later. There is a Jacobean, faintly Dutch flavour to the station house, which is built of local stone with brick quoins and splendid chimneystacks. The windows have lozenge-patterned panes, and BR's own adjective for it – 'cosy' – is well deserved.

Cambridge Station

Cambridge is almost the only large survivor of a type of station that was not uncommon in earlier days, a single-sided main platform for both directions, to and from which all trains require access by means of a 'scissors' cross-over in the centre. The advantage of this design is that only a single set of buildings is required for both directions of travel, and passengers and luggage require to use neither a bridge nor a subway, everything being accessible on the level. The disadvantage is of course the conflicting movements of trains which cause delays as they cross one another's path; also a great length of platform is required to accommodate two trains end to end.

Cambridge survives in very much the same state as when it was designed by the probable architect, Francis Thompson. There was originally a huge open *porte-cochère* of fifteen arches; this has been filled in to provide offices, but the arches are still a striking feature. There are some noteworthy decorative cornices and friezes in the public rooms. The whole building is simple and rather impressive.

An imaginative touch in recent years has been the restoration of the arms of the colleges of the University, in their correct heraldic colouring, above the arches of the *porte-cochère*.

Cambridge: the enclosed colonnade with the arms of the colleges

Chappel Viaduct, on what was formerly quite an important cross-country link (Colchester to Cambridge), now severely cut back

Chappel Viaduct

This structure illustrates vividly the part played by railways in the developing economy of East Anglia. Although it carries only a single-track line from Marks Tey (which formerly ran on as far as Cambridge but is now cut back at Sudbury), it was the longest viaduct on the former Great Eastern Railway (335 yards), with thirty-two arches. It is an impressive intruder into the placid agricultural scenery of the Stour Valley. It is also quite venerable, dating back to 1849, when it was built by the Stour Valley Railway, later absorbed into the GER.

Access: By car, take the A12 London–Colchester road and turn north onto the A604 at Ash Green, three miles east of Marks Tey and about five miles west of Colchester. The A604 gives an excellent view. OS map 155.

Felixstowe Station

East Anglia, as that part of England closest to the Netherlands, seems to have received a number of Dutch influences from across the North Sea. Waterways and windmills, and perhaps even the character of the inhabitants, show similarities, and this even includes railway architecture. The former Great Eastern Railway built a number of stations in which a Dutch or Flemish style appears. One of these is Felixstowe Town.

The Great Eastern Railway and its successor, the London & North Eastern, were energetic in promoting the tourist attractions of Felixstowe and, although its rail connection depended on a single-line branch from Ipswich, a rather grand station with four platforms was built here to accommodate through trains to London as well as the local services. Although today only a single platform is needed for the diesel shuttle to and from Ipswich, a visitor can well appreciate that the buildings are, to quote from *The Railway Heritage of Britain* 'one of the best examples of the GER Architect's Department's flirtation with end-of-century "Domestic" styling, with echoes of Norman

Felixstowe Station's imposing façade now hides a shopping centre – the trains are banished to a remote corner

Shaw in the combination of striped and plain Dutch gables, stone string-courses in the neat red brickwork and six-light window sashes'.

Fortunately, a major rescue operation on the station buildings has been undertaken. Apart from cleaning and repainting, the structure has seen interior remodelling, the concourse having been named 'Great Eastern Square', surrounded by shops and providing a spacious entrance lobby to a newly built and adjoining supermarket.

British Rail's shuttle diesel train to and from Ipswich has been banished to a stopping-place half-way down one of the former long platforms, and passengers now have quite a walk to the street past the new shopping centre. But it is good to see the formerly impressive station building once more in something approximating its appearance when it was the pride of the Great Eastern Railway, instead of one of British Rail's uncared-for orphans!

5. The North of England

Introduction

The rival counties of the Red and the White Rose have at least one thing in common: the rich variety of their landscapes and of their rail networks. Each county includes part of the Pennine range of hills – some would say, mountains – that forms the 'backbone' of England, together with fertile plains such as the Lancashire Fylde and the Vale of York. Industry is widespread in each county, yet each has also areas of great scenic beauty.

Railways came early to this region, starting in the industrial belts but soon driving up into the hills to link the cotton districts of Lancashire with the woollen districts of Yorkshire. No fewer than four main cross-Pennine railways were built, and the total network was shared between the London & North Western, the Midland, the Great Central, the Great Northern and the North Eastern. At one extremity of Lancashire the oddly named Cheshire Lines Railway and at another the Furness Railway were also to be found.

As one would expect, the cities that were joined by the world's first steam passenger railway, Liverpool and Manchester, are particularly rich in memorials of the early railways. But there is also an immense variety of structures of the 'Middle Ages' of the railways, when they expanded at a hectic pace to meet the demands of Victorian industrial expansion, from the massive classical façade of Huddersfield Station to picturesque ex-Midland Railway 'cottage Gothic' country stations. And the geography required the building of many viaducts and bridges, as well as the boring of tunnels – making this an altogether rewarding region to visit from the railway as well as other points of view.

The mountains of the Lake District presented a formidable barrier to the engineers planning the first railway linking England and Scotland on the west side of the country. George Stephenson favoured a 'water-level' route from Lancaster to Carlisle that would avoid gradients by means of a massive detour to the west, involving

How the railway looked to the citizens of Newcastle in 1848

greatly increased mileage. Eventually the railway was built on the
eastern edge of the Lakeland hills, over Shap Fell, by Joseph Locke; it
involved steep gradients, severely taxing the power of the early steam
locomotives; but it was a much shorter route than Stephenson's
coastal line, much of which was later built as a railway of chiefly local
importance, the Furness Railway.

Even though the heart of the Lakeland mountains was left
untouched, the Lakeland poets – Wordsworth, Coleridge and Southey
– complained about the railway in terms that might be used by
present-day conservationists. 'Is there no nook of English ground/
Secure from rash assault?' thundered Wordsworth. Later, Ruskin
added his voice to the earlier critics. (How they would have reacted to
the motorway one can barely imagine.) The railways today – even
though the electric wires of the 'overhead' have been strung along the

line crossing the bleak emptiness of Shap Fell – have merged with the landscape, in some cases even enhancing it.

East of the Lake District, the Settle & Carlisle Line, long threatened with closure as uneconomic, traverses the harsh uplands of the Pennines by a string of major engineering works which many people see as an outstanding example of Victorian enterprise and skill, something that should not be thrown on the scrap-heap, even though the railway no longer serves its original purpose as a third main Anglo-Scottish route, competing with both the East and West Coast lines. 'The Settle & Carlisle' has passionate defenders, who include railway historians, industrial archaeologists, architects and con-servationists. Although its train service (at the time of writing) is only a skeleton one, the line has potential value as an alternative route, in the event of either the East or West Coast main lines being blocked by a mishap; it has been used for this purpose more than once in the past. But its maintenance is expensive for BR, made worse by the heavy estimated cost of repairs to the line's greatest feature, the Ribblehead Viaduct. The dilemma of economics versus preservation is here specially acute.

Of all the regions of Britain, the North-East is perhaps the richest in railway memorabilia. Coming by train from the South, the entry into York is a splendid introduction to the tradition, the confidence and the wealth of the North Eastern Railway. York Station has a spaciousness and solidity all its own – until you go further and reach Newcastle, equally grand. It is a cliché that the North-East was the cradle of railways, but it is undeniably true. With little effort one can visit the Causey Bridge (or Tanfield Arch), the first major work of railway engineering. George Stephenson's birthplace is here, and the whole region is honeycombed with relics of the early railways, which were dedicated to the haulage of coal and which pioneered this form of transport. It is a bonus that so much of the landscape is grand, a fine setting for these efforts of the engineers.

A single railway company dominated the region after 1854, when the North Eastern Railway was formed from the combination of the York & North Midland, the York, Newcastle & Berwick and the Leeds Northern companies. It became highly prosperous from its huge freight traffic, especially coal; but it also catered well for its passengers, never skimping expenditure on stations or trains. It boasted a distinguished breed of railway managers (including one who later became a Cabinet Minister and First Lord of the Admiralty, Sir Eric Geddes, and a Chairman, Sir Edward Grey, later to be Foreign Secretary at the outbreak of the 1914-18 war) ... a lordly railway, which has stamped its individuality over the whole region.

The grandeur of the former North Western Hotel masks Lime Street Station, in Liverpool

From York Station, the heart of the North Eastern Railway, it is only a few minutes' walk to the National Railway Museum in Leeman Street – something to be visited by everyone with an interest in any of the many facets of our railways' history.

Liverpool (Lime Street) Station and Edge Hill Station

Many schoolchildren know something about the world's first passenger steam railway, the Liverpool & Manchester, and especially about the difficulties George Stephenson faced in carrying the line over the bog called Chat Moss. Less attention is given to the huge engineering works involved at the Liverpool end of the line: the deep cutting through red sandstone with near-perpendicular walls, called rather oddly 'Olive Mount', two miles long, at a maximum depth of a hundred feet. It included a 'Moorish arch', often illustrated in early prints of the Liverpool & Manchester Railway. From Edge Hill, on the city's outskirts, a tunnel was driven downhill to a central terminus for passengers at Crown Street. Another tunnel, the Waterloo Tunnel, was provided for goods traffic to the docks at Wapping. Through these tunnels trains had to be pulled by cable up to Edge Hill, the engine house for which is still visible on the south side of Edge Hill Station.

Crown Street was replaced by Lime Street in 1836, through a new tunnel from Edge Hill – since mostly opened out. Lime Street today is the result of considerable rebuilding in 1867 and 1874. The train shed

Liverpool Lime Street: an interior of the Hotel block (now sold) when it was for a time used as railway offices

is rather a fine structure of glass and ironwork; the frontage of the station is absorbed in the huge North Western Hotel, designed by Alfred Waterhouse in 1871. It is faintly reminiscent of that architect's vast Prudential Assurance building in London, apart from the use of stone rather than brick for its turreted and gabled extravagance.

The frontage of the hotel (no longer in BR ownership) has been cleaned recently; it well matches the impressiveness of the municipal offices and St George's Hall which are its neighbours.

Lime Street Station itself has been cleaned and imaginatively restored, and now deserves careful inspection.

Earlestown Station

After Liverpool and Manchester were joined by rail in 1830, obviously the next step was to join them both to Birmingham and London. For this purpose the Grand Junction Railway was authorized in 1833 to build a railway from Birmingham to the mid-point of the Liverpool & Manchester at Newton-le-Willows, with junctions facing in both directions, thus making a triangle. Although this triangle of lines later became much less important – with the opening of direct lines from Crewe to Manchester and from Weaver Junction to Liverpool – it remained a railway complex associated with the establishment later of the London & North Western Railway's wagon works. This was named after Hardman Earle, a Director of the Liverpool & Manchester Railway.

The passenger station at Earlestown, where the Manchester–Liverpool and Manchester–Warrington lines diverge, is interesting as it was built as early as 1840 by the Liverpool & Manchester Railway; the building, in the angle of the junction platforms, is an extraordinary example of early Victorian eclecticism in architecture, with its Tudoresque stone construction embellished with octagonal chimneys, crenellations, mullioned windows and carved exposed wooden beams in the interior.

Rainhill Skew Bridge

The boldness – and unconventionality – of the early nineteenth-century railway engineers is splendidly illustrated by the Rainhill Skew Bridge on the Liverpool & Manchester Railway. In the railway's thirty-three miles of route, no fewer than sixty-three bridges had to be constructed: the Rainhill Bridge, however, was unique in that it carried a main road across the railway at an angle of 34 degrees, and it is arguably the first masonry stone bridge at such a skew. It cost £3,735, and the rusticated sandstone of which it is built came from a local quarry. A full-size model is said to have been set up in a field

Extraordinary Tudor chimneys in a improbable situation at Earlestown Station

nearby, the stones afterwards being cut to correspond with the wooden blocks.

A tablet on each side of the bridge is inscribed:

Erected June 1829.
Charles Lawrence Esq
Chairman.
George Stephenson
Engineer.

The best-known illustration of the bridge as originally built is an etching by I. Shaw of Liverpool, No. 7 in a series of eight, showing a locomotive in 1831 passing under the bridge.

Access: By road, turn north off the M62 Liverpool–Manchester motorway at Junction 7. OS map 108.

Manchester (Liverpool Road) Station (closed)

The railways built in the first flush of enthusiasm for steam locomotion tended to be regarded as self-contained links – Stockton with Darlington, Liverpool with Manchester, London with

The historic Rainhill Skew Bridge by George Stephenson on the Liverpool and Manchester Railway, still standing and in use

Birmingham, and London with Bristol. Their termini were thought of as dead-ends. But very soon the concept of individual railways as part of a future national network began to take hold; early terminal stations were either abandoned or adapted for through running to other destinations. Curzon Street in Birmingham became a goods depot; Bristol (Temple Meads) had to be built – with difficulty – for London to Exeter, not just London to Bristol trains. And the prototype of them all, Manchester Liverpool Road, was soon turned over to goods traffic, so that through running between Liverpool and Leeds could be inaugurated via a new link and a new Victoria Station.

Luckily, Liverpool Road, though it is no longer in BR ownership, is the centre of a well-preserved complex of historic railway buildings; it recently came into its own with the celebrations marking the 150th anniversary of the Liverpool & Manchester Railway's opening. There is the original station façade with separate entrances for first- and second-class passengers. Further down the street are ex-railway offices, a goods shed built in the 1860s, and the original 1830 cotton warehouse in brick and stone – the real *raison d'être* of the L&M Railway's freight business, American cotton for Manchester.

Perhaps the most historic station of all: the first real passenger terminal in the world, Manchester (Liverpool Road)

Access: None by rail. Liverpool Road is in the north centre of Manchester, adjacent to Water Street on the east side of the River Irwell, which the railway bridged to reach the terminus.

Manchester (Victoria) Station

The Manchester & Leeds Railway was originally planned to end at a high-level terminus in Manchester at Oldham Road, despite the fact that it could not thereby form part of a major east–west through route, since the Liverpool and Manchester Railway, completed in 1830, had its terminus at Liverpool Road, $1\frac{1}{4}$ miles away and at a much lower level. After protracted argument, it was agreed to join the two lines in a new through station at Hunt's Bank; on 1 January 1844 the station was opened and, with royal permission, named after Queen Victoria.

The station has always been difficult to work, owing partly to the very steep gradients leading up from the east towards Miles Platting, partly to the immense variety of through, terminating and originating trains which it handles. It was completely rebuilt in 1884, and greatly enlarged again in 1903. It was formerly claimed to be the busiest station in Great Britain outside London. It had two unique features for many years: the longest single platform (2,194 feet), joining Victoria with the adjacent Exchange Station (now closed), and a remarkable overhead electric rail network, with suspended carriers, for transferring baggage and parcels to and from all points in the station. This also has disappeared.

The whole complex contains many points of interest, despite the effects of some 'simplification' of the train shed roofing by the LMS Railway between the wars and even more through wartime bombing. Still noteworthy are the Edwardian buffet, recently restored to its original décor, and the Lancashire & Yorkshire Railway wall map.

Manchester Victoria's past owners are commemorated below the clock

Most important, however, is the restoration of the main block fronting the street and dating from 1909, the architect being William Dawes. Here, British Rail, in conjunction with Greater Manchester Council, has cleaned the whole frontage and landscaped the area that became available following the demolition of the former offices opposite the station. The façade now appears in its original buff colour; particularly noticeable are the shell-shaped pediment with the clock and the gilt lettering 'Lancashire & Yorkshire Railway' (a delight to railway archaeologists) that is displayed twice along the façade. Those who remember Victoria Station only in its former dingy state can now visit it with some pleasure.

Manchester (Central) Station (closed)

The Great Train Hall, as it is now named, has become an exhibition and event centre. Greater Manchester Council and a private firm of developers are joint owners of the station, closed by BR in 1968. The Council purchased it for £1.5 million and found a commercial partner who worked on a scheme that attracted an £8 million Government grant. The total scheme was budgeted to cost £14 million.

The Midland Railway had a long struggle to reach Manchester, which it first achieved in 1867 over the metals of the Manchester, Sheffield & Lincolnshire Railway, using that railway's accommodation in London Road (now Piccadilly) Station. However, the Cheshire Lines Railway, in which the Midland and MS&LR were partners together with the Great Northern Railway, built the splendid Central Station in 1880. Its great train shed recalled St Pancras, and for many years it housed the Midland Railway's London–Manchester expresses, popular with many travellers for their excellent dining cars and the spectacular scenery of the Peak District through which the Midland line ran.

The train shed is only slightly less wide than that at St Pancras; it also has the pointed arch so characteristic of Barlow's design. The undistinguished range of wooden buildings that provided passenger facilities and offices was intended to be temporary; but they were never replaced before the station closed. It was a pity that the huge, ornate Midland Hotel did not complement the trainshed in the way that Sir Gilbert Scott's hotel in London complemented Barlow's great train shed there; the hotel is at a lower level and was formerly connected to the station only by a glass-roofed passage across the forecourt.

York Station and Railway Offices

George Hudson, the York linen-draper who became known as 'The Railway King' until his disgrace following the exposure of questionable financial dealings in some of the companies he controlled, had a maxim: 'Mak' all t'railways cum t'York.' Certainly he succeeded in this aim, because York is almost as much a railway centre as it is a cathedral city, a regional capital and a tourist attraction. Arriving in York by train, the sheer size and dignity of the station catch the imagination, with the sharply-curved arched roof of four great spans showing just how architectural ironwork can be. The decorative treatment, including Corinthian columns and quatrefoil openings, is well worth study, either from the platform or on the wide footbridge.

Outside there is a solid *porte-cochère* which is less grand perhaps

Overleaf: York Station's marvellous curving roof has seen everything, from early steam to modern diesels

than Dobson and Prosser's *porte-cochère* at Newcastle, eighty miles to the north. The station buildings of 1877 adjoin the great hotel, with its galleried staircase. A short distance away is the railway office building, built in a 'free' Edwardian version of Queen Anne or William-and-Mary architecture, the architect being Horace Field. Few railway headquarters offices have much distinction, but this building well reflects the prosperity and confidence of the North Eastern Railway which commissioned it in 1906. It now serves as the headquarters of British Rail's Eastern Region; its wide corridors and impressive board and committee rooms suggest spacious days when a generation of great railway managers was trained or accommodated here – Sir Eric Geddes, Sir George Beharrell, Sir Ralph Wedgwood, Sir Alexander Kaye Butterworth – not to mention eminent Directors such as Lord Grey of Fallodon. The North Eastern was a famous nursery of talent.

Before the present station was built, York was a terminus. The old station was almost opposite the present railway headquarters; trains reached it by passing through the old city wall in which a pointed arch was cut by the railway architect G.T. Andrews. In Tanner's Row the former station buildings were in 'Italianate' style. The train shed, after the station closed, was used for years as a Railway Museum; but after the National Railway Museum was built in Leeman Street and the exhibits were removed there, it was demolished and replaced by a block of modern railway offices, named Hudson House – a belated tribute to the fallen Railway King, whose native city had long ignored his memory.

National Railway Museum, York

For many years after 1925, York had a Railway Museum, housed in a former workshop and part of the old (terminal) station that closed when the great new through station was opened in 1877. It contained a number of notable locomotive and rolling stock exhibits in a relatively limited area. The main interest was in material from the predecessors of the London & North Eastern Railway, which had created the museum. There was also a smaller museum at Swindon, that had been established under the auspices of the Great Western Railway.

After nationalization the British Transport Commission created a larger Transport Museum at Clapham in South London in a garage building no longer required by London Transport. However, the 1968 Transport Act relieved the British Railways Board of responsibility for museum maintenance; in 1975 the Department of Education and Science opened a National Railway Museum at York,

The National Railway Museum at York has an unrivalled collection of exhibits

in a former motive power depot. The museum is formally constituted as an outpost of the Science Museum in London.

There is now a splendid collection (the largest in Europe) of locomotives, rolling stock and many other items of railway interest, ranging from the 1820s to the present day. In addition, audio-visual and film presentations are made, and a library is being built up, including records and photographs of historic importance.

A feature of special interest is that locomotives which are capable of being steamed are sent out on loan from time to time for train operation by approved organizations; this is facilitated by the museum's being rail-connected. Rolling stock movements in and out of the museum are greatly simplified by comparison with Clapham, where all the exhibits had to be moved by road.

The museum is open daily and special arrangements for parties can be made.

Knaresborough Viaduct
'Blind Jack of Knaresborough' is a figure of legend in transport history. The sightless engineer who laid out roads with unerring skill

would, later given vision, perhaps have conceded that the Leeds & Thirsk Railway had in 1848 embellished and not damaged his attractive native town with its splendid railway viaduct across the valley of the River Nidd. In fact, it could be taken for a Roman aqueduct or a medieval road bridge, with its construction of weathered stone and its fine castellated parapet. It is photogenic in the highest degree.

Access: By train from York, Leeds or Harrogate. By road, Knaresborough lies on the A59 which leaves the A1 at the York–Harrogate cross-roads. Alternatively, take the B6164 from the A1 at Kirk Deighton. OS map 104.

Huddersfield Station

To dwellers in the South of England, Huddersfield, sited in industrial Yorkshire, with today about 130,000 inhabitants, might seem an unlikely place in which to find a railway station of beauty, with a Grade I listing as a building of architectural value and historic interest. Even more surprisingly, the station was built not by one of the great and wealthy railway companies but by the Huddersfield & Manchester Railway, a useful link of some twenty-five miles in through communication between Manchester and Leeds but scarcely a great trunk line. However, the company commissioned J.P. Pritchett, architect to Earl Fitzwilliam of Wentworth Woodhouse, to build a fitting station at Huddersfield, and this he did in great style in 1847.

Huddersfield Station has happily been preserved and restored, even though the train service has declined somewhat. It is a splendid classical building with a frontage 415 feet long, consisting of a central portico supported by lofty Corinthian columns, with matching pavilions on either side, decorated with coats-of-arms. The dramatic quality of this station is heightened by its siting, between a long viaduct north of the station and the more immediately adjacent tunnels, south of the station.

The Manchester & Huddersfield Railway was absorbed by the London & North Western Railway in 1847, only a year after the LNWR was itself created through amalgamations, just before the station was completed. Fortunately, the later owners, including the London, Midland & Scottish which succeeded the LNWR in 1923, did not tinker too much with this majestic creation, and today BR has fully accepted the need to show it to advantage.

A combination of a dramatic townscape with a splendid railway viaduct, at Knaresborough

Perhaps the most impressive classical railway façade in Britain: Huddersfield Station

Hull Paragon's classical building luckily escaped the bombs which hit the train shed

Hull (Paragon) Station

Hull is not the least of the North Eastern Railway's fine stations. The first station in Paragon Street was designed by G.T. Andrews for the York & North Midland Railway and opened in 1848. It was a classical concept, 'a range of buildings of polished stone in front containing the offices, the central block distinguished by a colonnade – the station shed behind with iron roof in three spans', according to W.W. Tomlinson, the erudite historian of the North Eastern Railway.

In 1904 the North Eastern enlarged the station considerably; and in 1962 part of the enlarged building, a *porte-cochère*, was demolished and replaced by an office block through which the station is now approached. Happily, two main features of note survive: the original stone buildings by Andrews along the south side, and the booking hall with its huge carved oak circular booking office, the work of William Bell. The ceiling is noteworthy, especially for its huge lantern lights.

Paragon Station was lucky to escape major war damage when the surrounding area was largely devastated. On the night of 7 May 1941, during one of the heaviest of Hull's numerous air raids, the station roof was set on fire by incendiary bombs and was saved by four railwaymen who climbed onto the roof and extinguished the burning bombs.

Beverley Station

At one period in Britain's railway history, even wayside stations were often equipped with heavy all-over roofs, enclosing platforms, tracks and station buildings alike. Brunel built many such cosy structures of timber. The North Eastern Railway also favoured bringing its trains indoors, so to speak.

The cost of maintaining these massive structures, especially at stations where the traffic level is not high, has meant that many of them have been demolished, with platform awnings replacing their all-over roofs. But one outstanding example survives at Beverley, built as early as 1846 by the York & North Midland Railway, one of the constituents of the North Eastern Railway formed in 1854. Here the roof covering the platforms and tracks has hipped ends – not a very common feature. The station buildings, by the railway architect G.T. Andrews, are 'Italianate' in character, in yellow brick.

Beverley Station frontage is noteworthy for its delicate canopy

Lancaster (Castle) Station

It is interesting to note what short lives some early railway stations enjoyed before they were superseded. In Lancaster, for instance, the station built in 1840 for the Lancaster & Preston Junction Railway was replaced only six years later by a 'Castle' station which is still in use, though much extended in 1858, and again in the early years of this century. (The original station is now part of the nurses' home of the hospital.)

Sir William Tite, that prolific railway architect, built the first Castle Station for the Lancaster & Carlisle Railway when it became part of the main West Coast trunk route to Scotland. His symmetrical arcades were followed in 1858 by 'Castle'-like additions, including a tower and turret – all very suitable for this historic town and well worth a visit. The main entrance, however, is on the east or up side of the station, among buildings dating from 1900 to 1906 but still in keeping with the rest.

Ribblehead Viaduct

The history of the Midland Railway's push to the Scottish borders (in order to free itself of the constraints arising from the need to hand over to other railways its important traffic between the Midland Counties, Yorkshire and Lancashire, and Scottish destinations) epitomizes Victorian enterprise. Viewed by the narrow financial appraisals of today, it may have been barely justified; but the courage, faith and perseverance that built this railway between Settle and Carlisle can only be admired and wondered at nowadays.

Carrying a trunk line of railway through these savage uplands was a tremendous task for the railway's engineer, John Crossley (1813-79). Its thirteen tunnels and nineteen viaducts alone suggest the size of the task. The most spectacular single structure is the Ribblehead Viaduct, originally called Batty Moss Viaduct, 440 yards long, 165 feet in height, and with twenty-four semi-circular arches. Every sixth pier was specially strongly built, the idea being that, if any arch should fail, a maximum of six arches could follow suit. This precaution has not sufficed to prevent a demand from present-day engineers that the viaduct be strengthened at a cost that has thrown grave doubt upon the financial justification for maintaining the Settle & Carlisle line in operation, even though it remains a useful diversionary route in the event of closure of the West Coast main line, and has several times been proved a blessing on this account.

The line has two other claims for preservation: the beautiful scenery, albeit fearsome in winter, through which it runs, and the superb engineering of its major works. Various bodies have rallied to

Ribblehead Viaduct today, long threatened with closure

support its retention, including some preserved railway societies who
have operated scenic excursions, with steam traction, along its length.
Even British Rail has felt a pang at the prospect of throwing on the
scrap-heap so impressive a part of its engineering inheritance, and
has tried to whip up public financial support by advertising scenic
trips.

Access: Ribblehead Viaduct is eleven miles north of Settle Station and is the
first important structure on the way from Settle to Carlisle. By road, the
A682 follows the railway to Ribblehead from the south. OS map 98.

Skipton Station

Before the Midland Railway obtained its own main line to Scotland
via Carlisle, it was dependent upon its associate, the 'little' North
Western Railway which handed the Midland's Scottish traffic to the
'great' London & North Western at Ingleton. That did not matter
very much so long as the Midland's gathering and reception areas
were Yorkshire and the Midland counties, rather than London,
although in 1859 the Midland took a lease of the 'little' North
Western to make its position stronger. But with the opening of the
London extension in 1868, a through route from Settle to Carlisle
became desirable, if not essential; and the section of line pointing
north-west from Leeds and Bradford towards Settle became much
more important.

In 1876 Skipton was provided with a new station, built to the very individual Midland Railway standards. Happily, it survives today in quite good condition, despite the downgrading of the Settle & Carlisle Line. The first thing one notices from the street is the porch, with several arches and a stone panel displaying the Midland Railway's heraldic device, the mythical wyvern, emblem of the kingdom of Mercia. The stone-built station buildings behind are complemented by absolutely typical MR platform awnings, iron and glass in a ridge-and-furrow design with hipped ends and decorative cast-iron work in the shape of brackets, columns and finials.

Carlisle Citadel Station

Like Berwick-on-Tweed, Carlisle is an Anglo-Scottish frontier town with a long history of Border quarrels. Its railway station – arising from the need to end inter-railway disputes – is one of the select few that had a statutory basis, the Citadel Station Joint Committee, established by an Act of Parliament in 1873. The object was to afford rights to use the station to no fewer than seven railways that had from time to time previously been in dispute, sometimes acrimonious, about access. The railways were the London & North Western, the Caledonian, the Midland, the North Eastern, the Glasgow & South Western, the North British and the Maryport & Carlisle. Only the Transport Act of 1947, which nationalized the railways, wound up this curious organization.

The station exterior is one of Sir William Tite's most striking efforts in exploiting past architectural styles. It is a large Tudoresque composition with a massive entrance arcade; there is also a clocktower. Inside the station, one should notice particularly the fireplaces in the former refreshment room, and the picturesque bay windows overlooking the centre of the platforms, which formerly constituted the look-out of a station signal-box. The original design dates from 1847 when the two railways sharing in the cost were the Lancaster & Carlisle (amalgamated with the London & North Western in 1852) and the Caledonian; hence it followed that the other users were admitted more or less on sufferance until the Joint Committee was formed.

Morecambe (Promenade) Station

The mass exodus of workers from Lancashire and Yorkshire for their traditional holiday week – 'staggered' to prevent too much crowding and shortage of accommodation, town by town and county by county – has for many decades been centred upon Blackpool. Even more than Brighton, many years ago Blackpool rose to the challenge of mass

A splendid chimney piece in Carlisle (Citadel) Station's former dining-room

holidaymaking, and its techniques for coping – not to mention the character of its landladies – have passed into legend.

For those in the industrial areas who wanted something different, perhaps something considered superior, Llandudno and Morecambe were the favourite choices. Neither had the mass appeal of Blackpool: they might perhaps offer the sort of alternative in the North that Eastbourne offered to Brighton in the South.

The Midland Railway, which obviously served relatively few seaside resorts or towns, set about promoting Morecambe, on the shores of Morecambe Bay, as a popular resort. The first railway there was built in 1848 by the North Western Railway (not the LNWR but the so-called 'little' North Western) from Lancaster.

The Midland absorbed the 'little' North Western in 1857, partly in order to obtain an outlet to Scotland via the LNWR from Ingleton. The steamer service starting from Morecambe Bay had served Barrow (Piel Pier) and also Belfast; but the Midland transferred the Belfast

Grange-over-Sands Station epitomizes the pleasant character of the Furness Railway's architecture

sailings to nearby Heysham and concentrated on developing Morecambe as a resort attractive to visitors from Yorkshire and the Midland counties. It replaced the original NWR station in 1907 with a quite impressive affair called Promenade Station which had a fine glass-roofed concourse typical of the Midland's architecture.

The station buildings are a *fin-de-siècle* semi-Gothic design, in a warm stone colour, with particularly attractive quatrefoil decorations and a fine clock in a roof dormer. The *porte-cochère*, however, is an ironwork affair similar to a platform awning.

Grange-over-Sands Station

If Blackpool was the traditional holiday resort of the working masses of Lancashire and Yorkshire, with Morecambe and Llandudno one step higher in the social scale, then Grange-over-Sands came to represent everything that was quiet and select at the very top end. The Furness Railway's route there skirted the north side of Morecambe Bay, with its vast expanse of sand at low tide and the splendid backdrop of the Lakeland hills. The climate was mild, far removed from the bracing winds of Blackpool. As the resort became known following the arrival of the railway in 1845, a large hotel was built, followed by a new station in 1877, with adjacent gardens – all inspired by Sir James Ramsden, Managing Director of the Furness Railway.

The station could be in Cheltenham or Bath, or in any town where the well-to-do and the retired enjoy peace and orderliness amid pleasant scenery. It is built of local stone, with very attractive iron-and-glass platform awnings. The spirit of the Edwardian age lingers around it.

Wetheral Bridge

The Newcastle & Carlisle Railway was a venerable line, promoted in 1824, a year before the Stockton & Darlington was opened. Much longer (64½ miles) than the S&DR, there was nevertheless no problem in obtaining finance. The Act of Incorporation was obtained in 1829, but (a very important 'but') the company at its own wish was forbidden to use any 'locomotive or moveable steam engine' on the said 'railways or tramroads'.

The building of the railway involved some notable engineering works, of which probably the most important was the Wetheral Bridge, adjacent to Wetheral Station, just under four miles east of Carlisle. It was built by W.S. Danton from the designs of Francis Giles, the engineer to the company. It is 564 feet long, with five semi-circular arches of eighty-foot span, carrying the railway across the River Eden at a height of ninety-five feet. It was four years in building, being completed in 1834. The material used is local sandstone.

Access: Most trains between Newcastle and Carlisle call at Wetheral. By road, leave the M6 at Junction 43 East on to the A69, then turn South at Warwick for Wetheral. OS map 85.

Darlington (Bank Top) Station

Although lacking the venerability of Darlington North Road Station, Bank Top on the East Coast main line still has some historic interest. The first station was built here for the Great North of England Railway, united with others to join the North Eastern Railway in 1854. From Bank Top a link with the Stockton and Darlington terminus at North Road was also installed.

In 1887 the North Eastern Railway opened a modernized station, designed by William Bell, with a single large island platform with bays at each end. An unusual feature was that this fine through station was on a loop from the main line which bypassed it, thus avoiding any reduction of speed by non-stopping expresses.

The whole station, like York and Newcastle, expresses the solid self-confidence of the North Eastern Railway in its period of prosperity, when anything it undertook to construct would be carried through without the penny-pinching that afflicted some other lines. There are three spans of the lofty arched glazed roof, one covering the down tracks and down-side platform, another the central concourse and offices as well as the bay platforms, and the third the up-side platform and tracks. Screen walls close in the tracks on either side. The supporting iron columns are in the Corinthian mode. The whole station is effective and roomy; its lofty clocktower and handsome Dutch-style gables give a tone of impressiveness to the site.

For many years, from 1892 to 1924, George Stephenson's historic *Locomotion No. 1* stood on a plinth on one of the platforms at Bank Top Station; it now has a less exposed resting-place in the North Road Station Museum.

Darlington (North Road) Station Museum

Although the Stockton & Darlington Railway was opened in 1825, it was not until 1842 that it troubled to acquire a terminal station in the latter town; the reason for this was that the original concept of the railway was merely that of a specialized form of highway, like a canal or a turnpike road, open to all users on payment of the statutory tolls. However, the directors of the S&DR decided rather daringly to enter the carrying business as well, and on the opening day their steam engine, *Locomotion No. 1*, and 'the Company's carriage called the Experiment' were in operation. The company continued to haul coal and other merchandise thereafter, but for some time left the carriage of passengers to individual coach proprietors who fitted up vehicles with flanged wheels and drew them with their own horses.

This system of mixed traction (without any signalling!) led to unsatisfactory results – even occasionally to free fights as to who

The Stockton and Darlington Railway's terminus in the latter city — now mainly a railway museum

should take precedence at crossing points — and eventually the company decided to become the sole carriers, using their steam locomotives for that purpose. Now passenger stations were required — trains could not be stopped on request like a horse-drawn coach — and a terminus was built, some seventeen years after the date of opening, at North Road, Darlington.

The present station building is the second to have been constructed and is on a slightly different site from the original one. It dates from the 1840s and is a long, low building with a 'late Georgian' frontage. It is now closed to trains but accommodates the North Road Station Museum of exhibits illustrating the Stockton & Darlington Railway's history. *Locomotion No. 1* of 1825 and the later, six-wheeled *Derwent* locomotive are on display, together with S&DR rolling stock and many other relics.

Access: The museum is in Station Road, about three quarters of a mile north of the town centre. It is reached by taking the ring road to the north, leaving it by the A167 (called Northgate) and turning west into Station Road. OS map 93.

The splendid roof, with its reverse curve, at Newcastle Central

Newcastle (Central) Station

The curving steel and glass arches of this train shed recall York very strongly, though in fact they preceded York by some twenty-seven years. But it is perhaps the massive stone portico, even larger than the one at York, that most dramatically proclaims the self-confidence – and the wealth – of the North Eastern Railway; it has the grandeur that one finds in some great city stations on the Continent, but seldom in Britain. And it is truly 'central', an apt focus for the life of the city, approached at either end by striking railway bridges over the gorge of the Tyne: the King Edward VII Bridge, the main entry from the south, and the earlier High Level Bridge built by Robert Stephenson. Unquestionably the best way to enter Newcastle from the south is by train, when the view of all the Tyne bridges, including the new road bridge and the still newer Metro rail bridge, bursts upon the traveller's eye.

Leaving the station, everyone must be struck by the huge portico, designed by John Dobson, the station's first architect. Originally he intended to provide a 'noble' classic colonnade the whole length of the station along the south side of Neville Street. This was modified by a later North Eastern Railway architect, Thomas Prosser, partly in order to provide office accommodation in the station complex; nevertheless the frontage, 593 feet long, remains impressive, a tribute not merely to the North Eastern Railway but to its predecessors who united in promoting this as a joint station.

It was opened by Queen Victoria and Prince Albert in 1850, four years before the amalgamations that created the NER. An intriguing sidelight on the opening ceremony was a request by the Mayor of Newcastle that on that day all fires should be extinguished between eleven and two o'clock in order that the atmosphere might be free from smoke during the royal visit and ceremony!

High Level Bridge, Newcastle-upon-Tyne

The gorge of the River Tyne, separating Newcastle from Gateshead, for centuries presented a formidable obstacle and remained so even though road traffic could cross it by a low-level bridge after descending some hundred feet from the town centres on either side. A high-level, direct road bridge was long desired. Thomas Telford developed a proposal for one in 1825; later, plans were prepared by a Newcastle architect, John Green; but it was not until George Hudson launched the Newcastle & Berwick Railway, and included in its Parliamentary powers sanction for a Tyne bridge, that matters got under way. A separate High Level Bridge Company, financed by the Newcastle & Berwick and the Newcastle & Darlington Junction Railways, was set up to build a rail bridge to the designs of Robert Stephenson.

The bridge was 1,372 feet long, and its maximum height was 146 feet. Stephenson decided to provide six main spans, with smaller land arches on each side. The soil conditions for the foundations were unsatisfactory, and the piers, built of local sandstone, had to rest upon huge timber piles encased in concrete, the construction work having to be carried on within coffer-dams. This was the first recorded use of James Nasmyth's steam hammer for pile-driving; it was for both the coffer-dams and, later, the foundation piling.

For the main spans, 125 feet long, Stephenson faced a problem. First of all, the Parliamentary powers specified a road and rail bridge, and this implied two decks. Then, the question of using cast or wrought iron was important. Stephenson still had faith in cast iron, which other engineers, especially Brunel, were beginning to distrust. But he rejected the idea of cast-iron arches, and also the so-called compound girder consisting of a straight cast-iron beam strengthened

Robert Stephenson's original two-decker High Level Bridge across the Tyne gorge is still impressive, alongside its modern companions

by a truss of wrought-iron rods (very fortunately in the latter case, in view of the collapse of his Dee Bridge in 1847, built to this design). Instead, Stephenson selected 'bowstring' girders consisting of cast-iron ribs tied by wrought-iron chains, the upper (railway) deck being supported on cast-iron columns rising from the ribs of the arches. The road deck below, with pedestrian walkways, was supported by wrought-iron hangers, also connected to the columns, thus transmitting the load to the arch ribs.

The result is a most impressive structure, to be admired today even alongside the later railway (King Edward VII) bridge and the modern road bridge. Stephenson's bridge still seems the most original in design.

For many years the High Level Bridge brought trains into Newcastle Central Station at the east end, involving a reversal if they were continuing northwards. The King Edward VII bridge, opened in 1906, turned Central into a through station so far as the East Coast main line is concerned, and the High Level Bridge consequently lost much of its importance. One advantage of the change is that rail travellers can now obtain a good view of Robert Stephenson's masterpiece as they approach Newcastle.

Tyne & Wear Metro

It would be wrong to visit the North-East, even if in search of the railway past, and to ignore one of the most impressive examples of modern rail technology and architecture: the Tyne & Wear Metro, of which the first section was opened in August 1980, and the main route in November 1981 by the Queen. Major additions to the initial system – to be extended further in the future – were inaugurated in March 1984. The trains are light-weight 'rapid-transit' units, with driver-only operation. They chiefly utilize former BR routes around Newcastle and Gateshead but also some new tunnels under the city centre and a splendid new bridge across the Tyne. The stations are virtually unstaffed, and the whole system – points and signals – is fully computer-operated from a central control.

Most of the wayside stations are purpose-built, simple but adequate; but some former BR stations in the characteristic style of the North Eastern Railway are still in use and well worth inspecting: Tynemouth is an excellent example, and there are several others. A day spent touring Tyne & Wear Metro – avoiding peak-hour travel, of course – affords much of interest, including fine views of the sea and of the Tyne River gorge. And the Gateshead road-rail interchange station sets an example which other cities might well follow, from both the planning and the architectural aspect.

Monkwearmouth Station (closed)

Sunderland was originally linked to Newcastle-upon-Tyne by rail via the Brandling Junction Railway which ended at Monkwearmouth on the north bank of the River Wear, opposite Sunderland. The original station here, situated about a mile from Sunderland Bridge, was unimpressive, to say the least. One passenger suggested that it was kept so far away from the bridge in order to escape attention, as the wooden station shed covered only two carriages. In 1848, however, the line was extended to the river bridge, into a 'little stone-built station of classical design', in Tomlinson's words, a terminus until the railway bridge over the Wear was built in 1879.

The Brandling Junction Railway tried to make amends for its earlier cavalier treatment of its passengers with the permanent station, built in 1848 by the architect Thomas Moore. It is a gem – it has even been called a folly – worthy of a more important traffic location. Its main feature is a huge portico with Ionic columns, with wings and arcaded side walls – something which even the Earl of Burlington

The Queen Elizabeth Bridge built by the Tyne and Wear Metro contrasts strongly with Robert Stephenson's masterpiece nearby

Monkwearmouth Station when new

might have considered a suitable embellishment for his grounds.

In fact, it is now a museum, having been taken over for that purpose by the local authority; however, the railway flavour has not been lost, since there is a splendid period replica of a nineteenth-century booking office.

Access: By road, cross the Wear Bridge at Sunderland into Monkwearmouth. OS map 88.

Durham Viaduct and Station

Most railway viaducts are difficult to appreciate from the train, for obvious reasons. But the Durham Viaduct, in addition to being a fine structure in its own right, affords a splendid view of the city of Durham, with the cathedral and the castle crowning the conical hill encircled by the River Wear. Seen against a sunset sky, the view is unforgettable. One wishes that the train could pause there instead of in Durham Station, itself a pleasant stone-built Tudoresque edifice, probably designed by G.T. Andrews and dating from 1857. It has a castellated portico and mullioned windows.

Toiling up the hill to catch a train from this station, perched high above the river valley and the more modern parts of the ancient city of Durham, one can well appreciate its robust quality – and that of the stationmaster's matching house adjoining, affording superb views from some windows.

The viaduct, built at the same time as the station, is a listed building, Grade II. It is conspicuous, with its ten stone arches, from most parts of the city.

Royal Border Bridge

Berwick-on-Tweed has lived through a long, stormy history and still is very much a frontier town between England and Scotland. It long had a 'neutral' status and was named separately in legal documents along with the kingdoms of England and Scotland.

The London & North Eastern Railway rebuilt Berwick Station in red Dumfriesshire stone in 1927, replacing a mock-castellated Victorian building. This present station is substantial and quite handsome. But the chief interest in the locality is the splendid Royal Border Bridge, designed by Robert Stephenson and opened by Queen Victoria in 1850. The twenty-eight brick arches are faced with red stone, on stone pillars; the most striking feature, however, is the great

The splendid city of Durham is approached by a fine viaduct crossing the valley

Robert Stephenson's Royal Border Bridge has a splendid curve on the English side

curve at the south end, enabling the proportions of the bridge – it stands 126 feet above high-water level – to be appreciated from the train.

Access: By road, the best view of the bridge is obtained from the north bank of the River Tweed, reached by leaving the A1 by the town centre and descending near the railway station (signposted). OS map 75.

6. The West of England,
the Welsh Borders and Wales

Introduction

It is tempting to think of all the railways in the West of England as being of Brunel's creation; indeed today it is the routes of the former Great Western Railway that claim nearly all attention. It is easy to forget that the London & South Western Railway was formerly a strong competitor, thrusting west from Salisbury to Exeter, with a main line throwing off a string of branches to the Dorset and Devon coasts, and then curving north to serve Barnstaple and Ilfracombe with one arm, and Plymouth, Padstow and Wadebridge with the other. Today Southern Region hardly extends beyond Salisbury; the rest of its former West of England main line has been downgraded, much of it to single track; branches have been closed, and what remains is managed by the Western Region. The ghost of Brunel must surely smile at Dr Beeching's work.

There is a great deal to see and appreciate in Devon and Cornwall – Brunel's great Saltash Bridge still joins the two counties, though his numerous timber viaducts have been replaced by stone ones. Traces of his trial of the experimental Atmospheric System on the South Devon Railway can still be located, though practically all his stations with their overall timber roofs were rebuilt by the GWR in more conventional form at one time or another. But the West of England main line was the last stronghold of Brunel's Broad Gauge (7 feet $0\frac{1}{4}$ inch). It lasted there until 1892; reminders of it can occasionally be seen in the spacing of tracks, in relation to buildings or to each other.

The Welsh Borders are a mysterious country. On one side lies the prosperous and rather prosaic English Midlands; on the other, the mountains of Wales with their romantic quality. The railways of the region echo this 'frontier' feeling in the aspect of Shrewsbury Station, recalling a fortified Tudor manor house of the Marches. All the way from Chester to Hereford, stations, some half-timbered and others of stone, have a character of their own, as have the few remaining traces of the former Bishop's Castle Railway that led up to that curious little

ISAMBARD KINGDOM BRUNEL.

Born 9th April 1806.   Died 15th September 1859.

The genius of the West of England's railway system, in early middle life

hill-top town. Train services everywhere are not very frequent, and on the whole a car is desirable for exploration purposes.

Of Wales itself one can only say that the countryside dominates the railway, and it may be hard to concentrate attention on anything but natural beauties. But Robert Stephenson's Menai and Conwy Bridges are a 'must' in the north, as is the coastal line from Pwllheli to Machynlleth with its famous bridge crossing the Mawddach estuary at Barmouth, often featured in railway films.

Welsh railway stations as a rule are not remarkable, in comparison with their surroundings. One reason for this was the chronic poverty of the former Cambrian Railways which penetrated the Principality with two main lines crossing in scissors form – a fascinating railway in its day, though never a commercial success. Another, but very different, reason was the relative prosperity of the Great Western Railway which rebuilt its principal stations in South Wales (Newport, Cardiff and Swansea) in an efficient but rather characterless modern idiom.

The former independent railways that served the industrial valleys of South Wales – the Taff Vale, the Rhymney, the Cardiff, the Barry – all made their money (and a lot of it) from the coal traffic. Passengers were a secondary consideration, and their stations usually reflected this.

Lastly, the 'Great Little Railways of Wales', the narrow-gauge lines, mostly privately preserved, are unique and are all worth visiting: the Ffestiniog, the Talyllyn, and the sole British Railways remaining steam line, the Vale of Rheidol Railway based on Aberystwyth.

Box Tunnel

This is one of the great engineering works of the early railway age and a monument to the genius of I.K. Brunel. The tunnel is 1 mile 452 yards long, and on a falling gradient of 1 in 100. That led Dr Dionysius Lardner, an early railway statistician, to calculate that it was unsafe because, if the brakes were to fail, a train would emerge at a speed of 120 mph. Brunel was able to demonstrate that the eminent statistician had omitted to take into account the effects of friction and air-resistance, so that the emerging speed would be less than half the figure calculated by Lardner.

That the tunnel was fearsome to contemporaries is suggested by a story (often repeated but difficult to confirm) that, for some time after its opening, trains stopped on either side of the tunnel solely in order that nervous passengers could alight, travel by road to the far side and join a later train to continue their journey.

If Brunel had been faint-hearted, he might have given up, since flooding of the workings occurred several times. But he persevered and demonstrated his confidence by designing a massive tunnel entrance in classical style, using the beautiful Bath stone of the locality. The tunnel is absolutely straight: legend has it that, on Brunel's birthday and no other day, the sun shines through the tunnel from the east portal to the other one. But the legend is dubious; Brunel's birthday was 9 April, and the erudite historian of the Great Western Railway, E.R. MacDermot, records that the sun's rays are visible on or about 21 June.

Access: By rail there is no possible view other than a fleeting glimpse from a train window. By car, a view can be obtained by taking the A4 (Chippenham–Bath road) into the village of Box. OS map 172.

Bath: Sydney Gardens and Bath Spa Station

The traveller approaching Bath by train enjoys splendid views denied to the motorist. On the train's emerging from Box Tunnel, the streets and terraces of the city soon begin to appear, seen from a high level. Then the train threads its way beside Sydney Gardens along what might be a private driveway to some stately home. Brunel, with his usual sensitivity for the surroundings of his railways, met the demands of the difficult entry into the city alongside the Kennet & Avon Canal. He used the local Bath stone for attractive retaining walls and parapets, with three elegant road overbridges of great ornamental value. There are also two very short tunnels in this stretch of line, which is one of the few places where a passenger can count himself lucky if a train is stopped at a signal, since on the approach to Bath this provides an opportunity to appreciate an admirable stretch of ornamental railway.

Passing over the St James's Bridge, across the Avon, again offering a splendid panorama of the city, the train enters Bath Spa Station. The two platforms have heavy awnings of typical GWR type; from them staircases lead down to the main station building at street level. This looks straight down Manvers Street to the city centre and is also built of Bath stone, to Brunel's design. It is roughly Jacobean in style, with typical gables and an oriel window.

Brunel's sensitivity to the charm and character of Bath has unfortunately not been matched by other forms of transport, as the bus station just off Manvers Street demonstrates.

Access: This is one of the more rewarding sites to approach by train, as suggested above.

By road, Sydney Gardens, from which the railway features can be

Box Tunnel, which scared early travellers, had its portals built reassuringly solidly in Bath stone. Note the broad gauge tracks

The elegant approach by rail to Bath through Sydney Gardens

Bath Green Park: A splendid station, closed and now restored as an entrance to a supermarket

inspected at leisure, can be reached from the London direction, following the A4 on to the ring road, with the gardens on the east side; from the Bristol direction, the ring road can be followed into Pulteney Road, on the east of which the gardens are sited. OS map 172.

Bath (Green Park) Station (closed)

It is unusual to find a supermarket chain associated with a former railway station, but in Bath Messrs Sainsbury have done just this. Bath Green Park – formerly Queen Square – Station was shut in 1966 when the Somerset & Dorset Joint Line was closed, since it was the northern terminus of that straggling line from Bath to Bournemouth, as well as the point at which trains from Birmingham and the North reached the Somerset & Dorset, the most famous of these trains being *The Pines Express.*

The Midland Railway was the original builder. When it reached the city in 1869, by means of a branch ten miles long from Mangotsfield near Bristol, it decided to respect Bath's great architectural heritage. The architect of the station, J.H. Sanders, and its engineer, John Crossley, together provided a splendid classical building, with Ionic columns, elegant windows and a balustraded parapet. The glass-roofed train shed was also elegant, with side arcades, supported by columns on the platforms.

The Somerset & Dorset Railway arrived in 1874 and in the following year was taken over by the Midland and London & South Western Railways jointly. Between 1877 and 1930, its head offices were in Green Park Buildings nearby. These former offices were destroyed in an air raid in April 1942, although the station escaped, apart from the glass in the train shed roof which was not replaced until recent restoration work.

In 1971 the closed station became a listed building, Grade II, and the following year Bath City Council purchased it. Some immediate protective work was undertaken and, after various alternative proposals had been considered and two public enquiries held, an agreement was reached with Messrs Sainsbury and the British Railways Board for the erection of a supermarket on former railway territory beside the station, together with renovation of the station building. A great deal of work was involved.

Today the station is very fully restored, including former waiting-rooms, booking office, parcels office, refreshment rooms and so on. One interesting corner is the 'Footwarmers Room' where those useful articles were made ready for placing in compartments in the days before steam carriage-heating came in.

The train shed has been converted into a hall, with seating for about

750, that can be used for concerts and other performances. Sainsbury's store is at the back, on land formerly used for various railway purposes.

Access: Green Park Station is on the west side of the city, at the junction of Green Park Road and Charles Street, both of which constitute part of Bath's ring road – one-way circulation for the most part, and entered from the London direction off the A4 after the Walcot Street roundabout; from the Bristol direction, off the A4 at the Queen Square one-way system leading into Charles Street. OS map 172.

Bristol (Temple Gate and Meads) Stations

When the Great Western Railway was opened from London to Bristol, its terminus in Temple Gate was designed by I.K. Brunel with a castellated frontage in Bath stone and a wooden roof resembling the hammer-beam roof of the historic Westminster Hall. But in fact Brunel's pairs of beams are joined at their apex in a wide angle, and their thrust is taken by the iron columns which form arcades on either side of the 'nave' of this unique building.

The offices originally contained a board room, as the GWR directors met in both Bristol and London: the street frontage on Temple Gate is mock-Elizabethan, and a staircase led from street level up to the platforms at first-floor level.

Closely following the GWR, the Bristol & Exeter Railway, absorbed in 1876 by the GWR, built its own terminus, a wooden affair of much less importance, at a right angle to the GWR station – a sharp curve with a single platform providing a connecting link for through trains. Later the Midland Railway arrived and built its own terminus.

The resulting confusion led to the building of Temple Meads Station (1865-78), with a new and very impressive curved arched roof covering new platforms that swept round to link the GWR and B&E main lines. A new frontage block was built at right angles to the original Brunel façade, the architect being Sir Thomas Digby Wyatt.

Yet again, in 1932-5, further alterations were made in connection with the construction of additional platforms outside the all-over roof. Wyatt's façade was altered, especially the central tower, and new offices were built on the site of the old B&E station.

Today, in the approach road to the station, one sees the disused old Brunel station, now undergoing restoration by the Brunel Engineering Centre Trust, on the left-hand side; in the centre, Wyatt's impressive façade with the splendid curved train shed beyond; and on the right-hand side an office block dating from 1852, built for the Bristol & Exeter Railway in Jacobean style, the architect being S.C. Fripp.

Bristol (Temple Gate): the original terminus of the Great Western Railway

The whole complex deserves an unhurried visit which will reveal many interesting details, for instance the mullioned windows of the refreshment room on Platform 3.

Starcross Pumping Station

For a few years in the 1840s, many railway engineers were interested in Clegg and Samuda's 'Patent Atmospheric System' of railway traction. The idea was deceptively simple: to attach trains to a piston travelling along a pipe laid between the rails, with a longitudinal slit (closed and opened by movable flaps) through which the piston could be coupled to its train. Thus the train could be 'sucked' along by steam pumps which would create a partial vacuum in front of it. The system was obviously clean and silent, and the power that could be exerted depended quite simply on the size of the pumps. The basic principle was akin to that of electric traction, in which the power available is not limited to that of a locomotive but only to that which the generating stations can produce.

Experimental lengths of railway were equipped with this system at various places – on the West London Railway, in Ireland on the Dublin & Kingstown Railway, and on the Croydon & Epsom Railway.

However, the Prince Consort, always interested in new scientific

Pumping station at Starcross for the Atmospheric Railway

ideas, once asked George Hudson his opinion of the system, to which the 'Railway King' replied bluntly, 'I think it's a humbug, Your Royal Highness.' Hudson was not far from the truth, and it is surprising that Brunel, with his combination of practical grasp and visionary genius, was temporarily so fascinated by this system that he persuaded the directors of the South Devon Railway to adopt it, and the whole twenty-six miles from Exeter to Newton Abbot were so equipped. The trains certainly accelerated well and ran quite fast at the outset, but there were serious difficulties with points and crossings where the piston had to emerge from one tube and enter another. The fatal flaw, however, was the impossibility of keeping the tube sufficiently airtight for any length of time, when the flap valves closed after the piston had passed.

The South Devon trains ran 'atmospherically' for a couple of years; but operating problems and leakage, due mainly to incurable deterioration of the leather used in the flap valves, forced Brunel to give up, and steam locomotives took over.

To house the pumping engines, a string of ten engine houses was constructed, all in the 'Italianate' style then in favour, much used later for water-supply undertakings. The best survivor is probably that at Starcross. As one would expect from Brunel, it is well built, in sandstone, with attractively shaped doors and windows beneath a pantiled roof.

Access: It is now in private ownership, but a good impression of the exterior can be obtained from trains between Exeter and Dawlish, or from the A379 between Exeter and Teignmouth. OS map 192.

Saltash Bridge

Although Cornwall may not be considered as separate a component of the United Kingdom as Scotland, Wales or Northern Ireland, nevertheless on entering it the traveller is conscious of its strongly individual character. This feeling of passing a frontier when one traverses the River Tamar at Plymouth is splendidly emphasized by Brunel's Saltash Bridge (as it is generally known, though its official title is the Royal Albert Bridge). He built it for the Cornwall Railway that carried the line westwards from the South Devon Railway's terminal in Plymouth.

Brunel here faced the same demand from the Admiralty as Robert Stephenson had ten years earlier with his Menai Bridge, namely for a hundred feet of headroom at high tide. Like Stephenson, he turned to the use of wrought-iron tubes; but instead of putting the railway through two box-section members, always original in his approach to a problem, he suspended it from two huge oval tubes, curved and

Brunel's last masterpiece, the Saltash Bridge linking Devon and Cornwall

joined at their ends in a way that not merely gave the best stressing but was also aesthetically very pleasing. Each tube was 461 feet long; its cross-section was sixteen feet by twelve, and each weighed 1,060 tons. Each span was fabricated on the Devonshire side of the river and was floated to the site at high tide, being allowed to settle on the stone piers by the ebb. Thereafter the tubes were gradually jacked up and the stone piers built up beneath them – a slow process, as half the river had to be kept clear at all times. The first span was in place in 1857, the second in 1858, and the bridge was completed in time for opening by Prince Albert in 1859.

The portal arch bears the simple but proud inscription in large letters: 'I.K. Brunel, Engineer, 1859.' It was sad that Brunel was then dying and only saw his masterpiece complete from a couch placed on a flat truck, slowly propelled over the bridge by a locomotive. The railway company put up the inscription soon after Brunel's death.

Access: Even by rail, since the bridge is crossed at fairly low speed, some impression of its grandeur can be obtained. By road, it can be viewed from the adjacent road bridge (toll) on the A38 leading out of Plymouth. Side roads from the A38 lead down to the banks of the Tamar below the bridge, which is the best way to appreciate its quality. OS map 201.

Great Malvern Station

One of the pleasures of station-spotting on BR (as opposed to train-spotting) is the fact that none of the former railway companies ever evolved a really standard station building, still less, perhaps fortunately, a prefabricated one. Certainly, groups of stations by the same architect, such as Tite's for the Portsmouth Direct Line or Francis Thompson's for the North Midland Railway do show a strong family likeness, but no two are quite identical. These virtues of variety often lead to a station's reflecting the special character of a town which also has its own clear identity. Reinforcing this relationship, there are also some attractive examples here and there of planned development around a station, such as the gardens at Grange-over-Sands and, even more outstandingly, at Great Malvern.

The town had become a spa (and remains one, though today more Malvern water is exported than is drunk at its source) long before the railway arrived in 1860. The stone-built station is described by BR as 'a fantasy of French Gothic motifs delicately applied to doors, windows, gables, dormers and chimneys'. French influence is certainly seen in the fleurs-de-lys on the iron railings and quatrefoils on the roof. Flowers and leaves appear on the cast-iron columns which support the platform awnings. It stands amid gardens with a landscaped approach road. The architect of this pleasing arrangement of buildings and surroundings was E.W. Elmslie.

Great Malvern Station and Hotel in the palmy days of the Spa

Shrewsbury Station

Shrewsbury city, protectively encircled by the River Severn, has always had something of a frontier character, as the naming of its Welsh Gate and English Gate suggests. This character extends to its railway history: the Great Western Railway's struggle to reach Liverpool by extending from Oxford and Wolverhampton came to a halt here. A compromise with the strongly entrenched London & North Western was reached at Shrewsbury. Joint ownership of Shrewsbury Station and of several lines in the area was the price of peace, though the GWR secured its own access to Chester before again having to come to terms over the next section as far as Birkenhead, leaving Liverpool tantalizingly remote on the other side of the Mersey.

The station, close to the Norman castle built to subdue the Welsh, was originally constructed in 1848 by no fewer than four companies that were later to merge into the LNWR, the GWR or the joint lines. They were the Shrewsbury & Birmingham (later GWR), the Shrewsbury & Chester (GWR), the Shrewsbury & Hereford (joint) and the Shropshire Union (LNWR).

The station is partly built on a bridge across the River Severn; its Tudor frontage could be that of an Oxford or Cambridge college. It is built in grey stone, with a parapet and battlements; its substantial clocktower contains an oriel window. The only distraction is the massive awning which spoils the composition of the impressive façade.

The architect was T.K. Penson, and the building is listed, Grade II.

Gobowen Station

The Shrewsbury & Chester Railway, which built the station at Gobowen in 1846, was at the heart of the bitter struggle between the Great Western Railway, with its battle-cry of 'The Broad Gauge to the Mersey', and its strong antagonist, the London & North Western. The key to victory was held by two small railways, the Shrewsbury & Birmingham and the Shrewsbury & Chester. After a long struggle, the Great Western managed to acquire both the 'fighting Shrewsburys'; but Parliament, in granting the amalgamation in 1854, stipulated that the narrow gauge should be retained, so the GWR won something of a Pyrrhic victory, and the extension from Chester to the Mersey had to be joint with the LNWR.

At Gobowen, eighteen miles north of Shrewsbury, the station was built in what BR describes as a Florentine style – perhaps a *palazzo* in miniature? It is stucco-faced, with a charming rounded bay at the end

Shrewsbury Station; largely restored but further restoration to come

Chester's grandiloquent façade showed early railway architecture at its best

with curved windows. Two storeys high, it has attractive, round-headed windows on the first floor and in the turret which balances the bay at the other end.

Chester Station

During the long war of attrition between the Great Western Railway and the 'Euston Square Confederacy' caused by the GWR's ambition to reach the Mersey from Paddington, Chester, like Shrewsbury, was one of the main battlegrounds. The GWR had supported the small Shrewsbury & Chester Railway, while the Chester & Holyhead Railway was an associate of the London & North Western Railway, which was to absorb it in 1858.

Despite the competing ambitions of their powerful backers, these two small railways did manage to agree upon the construction of a joint station at Chester, in 1848, for which the architect was Francis Thompson. Later, since the peace terms included joint ownership of the Chester & Birkenhead line, the Great Western's dream of an independent, fully owned GWR route to Liverpool (and even to Manchester) from Chester came to an end.

Chester Station is a surprisingly large structure (the frontage block exceeding a thousand feet in length), in brick with stone dressings and sculptured decoration. The style is strongly Italianate, with a pair of towers resembling *campanili* above a central portico with arches, flanked by arcades ending in lower turrets. The Italian character is emphasized by the use of pantiles for the roof.

Renovation has been carried out recently by means of a joint scheme between the British Rail Property Board and a firm of local architects, who now have their office in one wing of the building. Fire damage had to be repaired, and skilful restoration of the exterior coupled with remodelling of the interior was involved.

Oswestry Station (closed)

Oswestry was formerly the headquarters of the Cambrian Railways, which straggled through Central Wales for many years, performing a useful public service but unable to earn sizeable profits and finally absorbed in the GWR in 1923.

At Oswestry the Cambrian headquarters building was erected in 1866 or thereabouts: it is in the Italianate style so popular with railways at that date, basically in brick with stone dressings; the bay windows are a good feature.

The station and offices are – sadly for Wales – now closed.

Access: The A4083 (a spur from the A5 trunk road, which avoids Oswestry on its way from Shrewsbury to Chirk) leads into the town; the former station is on a short side-turning to the east of the town centre. OS map 126.

Oswestry Station was a small railway company's headquarters in its day

Welshpool Station was also a railway company headquarters for a time

Welshpool Station

This surprisingly large and impressive building dating from 1860, in French Renaissance style (a sort of *château* in rather improbable surroundings), is more than a station. It was for a time the headquarters of the Oswestry & Newton Railway, which merged with the Mid-Wales Railway to form the nucleus of the Cambrian Railways, that interesting if impecunious system that was the backbone of transport in Central Wales for many years.

Cardiff (Bute Road) Station

The independent South Wales railways that ran from the coast up the coal-mining valleys were not as a rule inclined to spend much money on imposing passenger stations. Their profits came from hauling heavy coal trains downhill, and the empty wagons uphill, a transport economist's dream! No wonder the Taff Vale Railway, the largest of the coal lines, had paid $17\frac{1}{2}$ per cent frequently before the 1914–18 war.

From these resources, the Taff Vale built one substantial passenger station at Queen Street, Cardiff, which in its heyday handled 16,000 passengers a day. Nearby were the head offices of the railway company, including a splendid board room that would not have

Cardiff (Bute Road) was originally the Docks terminal of the prosperous Taff Valley Railway – honoured by being designed by Brunel

disgraced the headquarters of the Great Western Railway which swallowed up the Taff Vale in 1923. Today Queen Street lies on a pay-train route which terminates nearer the docks at a venerable station formerly known as Cardiff Docks.

This latter is historic in that it was built as early as 1840, and the engineer to the company was I.K. Brunel. The docks station, now known as Bute Road, is a handsome two-storeyed stucco building, very characteristic of its period; it could well be in Brighton or Cheltenham. It is a listed building, Grade II.

Machynlleth Station and Talerddig Cutting
The Mid-Wales railway line which links Shrewsbury with Aberystwyth was built in stages. The eastern portion was the Shrewsbury & Welshpool Railway (GWR and LNWR joint) but the western portion was built by independent companies, later joined in the Cambrian Railways. The section from Newtown to Machynlleth passes through much wild country before descending to the valley of the Dovey. At Talerddig the line is 693 feet above sea-level, reached by a gradient as steep as 1 in 52, and the summit contains a cutting no less than 120 feet deep through solid rock, excavated after the original idea of a tunnel had been dropped. Its depth is a record for Britain. It

has another claim to fame: the contractor was David Davies, who found the stone excavated here was suitable for use in adjacent railway structures and who is said to have invested the profits derived from this contract in coal mining in the Rhondda Valley so as to lay the foundations of the Ocean Collieries empire which made him the leading business tycoon of South Wales for many years.

Machynlleth Station is as remarkable as Talerddig Cutting for both its history and its architecture. The start of the work on the railway in November 1858 was an occasion of great local festivity, with processions and banners. The workers took part in the former, described in the programme for the ceremony as following in procession the second of three brass bands under the headings of 'Miners and Quarrymen, headed by their Captains, all wearing Sashes'. The proceedings went on to 'a generous imbibing of Mr Lloyd's prime port, sherry, etc' by the upper classes, whilst the 'Miners and Quarrymen ... dined at the house of Mrs Margaret Owen, the White Lion Inn, perhaps the most noted house in the county for the excellence of its ale'.

This auspicious gastronomic beginning led to the opening, five years later at the completion of the railway, of a station of great charm. It looks like a row of cottages built of the local stone, with three symmetrical gables embellished with highly decorative bargeboards and finials. For a short time, until the railway became part of the Cambrian Railways in 1864, its head office was located here.

Dovey Junction

Rather like Trent, Dovey Junction is a railway station without a hinterland – it exists in the middle of nowhere and was built for railway operating purposes rather than for passengers or freight. Unlike Trent, however, it is situated amid scenery of great beauty and grandeur. There is also to be seen a timber viaduct somewhat resembling the much longer one over the Mawddach estuary at Barmouth not far away.

Access: By the A489 road from Machynlleth to Aberystwyth. OS map 124.

Menai and Conwy Bridges

Every visitor to North Wales should view these striking bridges, built by Robert Stephenson for the Chester & Holyhead Railway almost simultaneously, although the Conwy Bridge was finished first, in 1849; the Britannia Bridge in the following year. Both bridges were built in a unique form, namely wrought-iron tubes through which the rails were laid, to cross the Menai Strait and the River Conwy. Stephenson was attracted by the strength afforded by the tubular

The spectacular cutting at Talerddig is the deepest in Britain

Machynlleth Station – dating from 1863, built by the Newtown and Machynlleth Railway

form, which offered a solution to the Admiralty's demand for a clear headroom of 105 feet above high-water level, very difficult to obtain with an arch form of construction.

The Conwy Bridge, required at the same time for completion of the railway, enabled Stephenson to establish that the tubes could be self-supporting, without needing suspension chains. It comprised two parallel tubes of 400 feet clear span; these were floated out on pontoons and raised by hydraulic presses, to rest on the piers. The latter were given a castellated finish with battlements, to harmonize with Conwy Castle, through whose walls the railway was to run.

The Britannia Bridge was a more difficult and ambitious project, with each of two tubes including 230-foot and 460-foot spans supported on three piers. Towers suggesting an Egyptian temple framed the railway entrance to the tubes, with couchant lions on their tops – a fine piece of bravado, for which the engineer was helped by Francis Thompson as architect and John Thomas as sculptor.

Raising the tubes was a tricky operation, owing to the tides in the Menai Strait. Stephenson insisted upon each lift being strictly limited

A contemporary design sketch of Robert Stephenson's fine Conwy Bridge

An artist's design for the portal of Stephenson's Menai Bridge

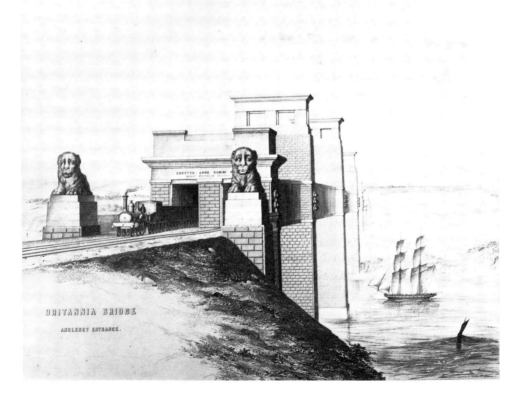

to a few inches until the piers could be built up to constitute a permanent support. Even so, one hydraulic press gave way and a tube dropped, causing the death of a workman.

The bridge stood, much admired, for 120 years. In 1970 a disastrous fire, accidentally started by two schoolboys, ignited the timber linings of the tubes and the heat weakened the ironwork to such an extent that the bridge had to be largely reconstructed. The tubes were removed and replaced by the two present steel arched spans, though of course the towers stand as before. The opportunity was taken to convert the bridge to a road and rail link, though the roadway is above the railway, not below it as in the case of Robert Stephenson's High Level Bridge at Newcastle-upon-Tyne.

Access: By rail, the bridges cannot be fully appreciated. By road, the A55 from Chester to Holyhead gives a good opportunity to view. OS map 115.

7. Scotland

Introduction

In many ways the railways of Scotland match the scenery and even the history of their country. No station is more romantically situated than Edinburgh's Waverley, in the gorge between that splendid city's Old Town and the New Town, and flanked by Princes Street Gardens. Glasgow's fine Central Station seems to illustrate the confidence of the commercial capital; coastal stations such as Wemyss Bay, spacious and airy, typify the former Caledonian Railway's sedulous concern about appearances and orderliness; whilst echoes of Scottish baronial architecture are dotted all over the railway system.

Scottish railway history is as distinctive as its architecture: the rivalry between the men of the Glasgow & South Western and of the Caledonian was a clan feud, no less, with the 'Caley' known to all the men of the 'Sou' West' as the 'Auld Enemy' – very different from, say, the English London & North Western's genteel disdain for its Midland Railway competitor. There was a time when the Aberdonians delighted in despatching the mail train to Inverness only seconds before the passengers arriving by the supposedly connecting train from the South could board it – incidentally, one reason for the Highland Railway being built to bypass Aberdeen!

Touring Scotland by car will bring one to a number of notable sites, from the Forth Bridge seen from below, or the great Glenfinnan Viaduct at the head of Loch Shiel, to clean and well-tended country stations in Ayrshire and Angus. But arriving by rail is a notable experience: the splendid view from the train crossing the Royal Border Bridge, or the coastal scene as the *Aberdonian* swings down from the cliff-top overlooking the grey North Sea and rounds the curve by the Nigg lighthouse to enter Aberdeen, is not easily forgotten.

Sadly, one or two of the most scenic and architecturally appealing railway routes are now closed. Above all, the loss of the 'Waverley Route' from Edinburgh to Carlisle through the splendid country of the upper Tweed is to be regretted, though fortunately Melrose Station is being restored as a private house. Sad also is the closing of the 'Port Road', the direct line from Carlisle to Stranraer of the former Portpatrick & Wigtownshire Railway. Boat trains from England for the ships to Ulster now make a long circuit by way of Kilmarnock. Another sad closure is that of the Deeside line from Aberdeen to Ballater. The closing and demolition of that grand terminus, St Enoch Station in Glasgow, has also been a serious loss. But there is still a vast amount to be seen and enjoyed, not merely in the Highlands or in Galloway but also in the industrial belt of Central Scotland and in the North-East. Hopefully, too, some threatened routes such as those leading to Fort William and Mallaig, from Inverness to Wick and Thurso, and to the Skye ferry at Kyle of Lochalsh, now seem to have a more secure future, partly on political and partly on economic grounds.

Dumfries Station
The Midland Railway's Scottish close associate, the Glasgow & South Western Railway, shared many of the characteristics of its English partner. It had a deadly rival in the Caledonian, just as the Midland had with the London & North Western. Both railways traversed much beautiful if wild scenery; both were interested in the Anglo-Irish traffic; and their main termini in Glasgow and London both had magnificent, arched, glass-and-ironwork train sheds.

Similarities could also be found in the neatness of their stations and the elegant ridge-and-furrow glass awnings over the platforms, supported on decorative cast-iron columns. Dumfries Station is an excellent example: it would look at home in Derbyshire.

The main station building is a solid red sandstone two-storey block, typical of the architecture of this fine, clean town. It is enhanced by two well-balanced single-storey wings. It is a listed building, Grade B, built in 1859.

Kilmarnock Station
This is an impressive station, bearing in mind the relatively light train service today over the former Glasgow & South Western Railway's main line to England. Two sets of buildings are worth noticing on the down platform: those of the original station dating from 1843, and the additions in 1877-8. The earlier work is in light-coloured sandstone – the later in red sandstone. The station's presence is made known in the town by the clocktower with a roof pediment.

When the later additions were almost complete, in 1877, the *Kilmarnock Standard* was eloquent in praise of the railway. A long and

Very 'Midland Railway' in appearance is the station at Dumfries

detailed account of the railway installations in the town concluded that 'the *coup d'oeil* of the whole is exceedingly pleasing and agreeable'. BR's predecessor, the G&SWR, obviously had a good public relations man!

Wemyss Bay Station
The former Caledonian Railway was uncompromising in its insistence upon good design, good materials and good maintenance for its passenger stations. This was in considerable contrast to its competitor, the North British, which had often sought economy at the expense of

The former Caledonian Railway's dignity and seemliness are splendidly exemplified at Wemyss Bay – graceful, spacious and, above all, tidy

seemliness in its older stations. Even for the 'Caley', however, Wemyss Bay Station was outstanding. It was, of course, a major point of embarkation for the railway's Clyde steamers, taking well-heeled Glasgow commuters home as well as excursionists enjoying a day 'doon the watter'. As a show-piece it was often photographed, though the interior is aesthetically more important than the exterior.

The platforms are gently curved and end in a spacious concourse containing a circular booking hall, and lit by fan-light glazing. Traditionally the concourse is embellished throughout the summer with hanging baskets of flowers, lovingly tended in the best Scottish gardening tradition.

Outside, the station is cosy rather than grand: the style has been described as 'Domestic Revival', with half-timbering and gables rather reminiscent of many suburban villas, but based on substantial sandstone footings. The Chief Engineer who became General Manager of the Caledonian, Donald Mathieson, had a good deal to do with the design, attributed officially to the company's architect, James Miller.

Leadhills Viaduct

It is perhaps surprising that Scotland was not provided with more 'light railways' to open up sparsely populated districts. However, one such line ran from the Caledonian Railway's Carlisle-Glasgow main line at Elvanfoot to Leadhills, the highest village in Scotland, and Wanlockhead. Between the latter two places, a remarkable viaduct was constructed in brick and concrete – a very unusual combination of materials for a railway structure at that date (1902). Moreover, the bridge is on a curve; its eight spans make it an impressive sight.

Access: None by rail. From the A74 Carlisle–Glasgow road, the B7040 from Elvanfoot leads to Leadhills. Alternatively, the B797 from the A76 Dumfries–Kilmarnock road, just south of Sanquhar, leads to Wanlockhead and Leadhills. OS map 71.

Waverley and Haymarket Stations, Edinburgh

The exterior of the only remaining terminus in Scotland's capital is not striking, but the site is highly romantic, lying in the dry valley between Edinburgh's New Town and the Old Town, flanked by attractive sloping gardens and the distinguished façades of Princes Street. Not many stations allow the train passenger to emerge into the very heart of a city simply by climbing a flight of steps; but the Waverley Steps are probably the windiest place in a windy city. When encumbered by luggage, the passenger feels like an Alpine climber by

A remarkable Scottish viaduct built in brick and concrete at Leadhills

the time he reaches Princes Street!

The train shed of Waverley is quite impressive. There is a single huge island platform with offices in the centre and bays at each end, all covered by a good glass roof supported on decorative Corinthian iron columns. The whole is enclosed within curtain walls of ashlar stone. The symmetry of the design was a little spoilt when a narrow subsidiary island platform for local traffic was added outside the curtain walls.

The station was the pride of the North British Railway, which was not otherwise noted for lavish expenditure in these directions. This pride was best expressed in the fine booking hall with its decorated glass dome and ceiling.

The North Bridge linking Princes Street with the Old Town is a fine structure crossing directly over the station, to which it gives access by carriageways.

Haymarket was the original terminus of the Edinburgh & Glasgow Railway, built in 1842, before the link with the Edinburgh & Berwick was built. Extension from Haymarket to the Waverley site and construction of a proper through station took a long time and aroused much controversy in view of the special value of the site. The Haymarket Station block is a fine, stone-built, classical building with a portico supported by Doric columns, the whole surmounted by a clock above the cornice. But at platform level Haymarket is a pretty austere place since it lost its overall roof, dating from 1842, now preserved elsewhere.

Forth Bridge

Scotland might have had a bridge disaster in the Firth of Forth instead of the Firth of Tay if Sir Thomas Bouch's 1873 design for a huge suspension bridge over the Firth had been completed. Work had actually started when the Tay bridge collapsed, and with it Bouch's reputation.

A totally different design was prepared, incorporating three huge cantilever spans, by Sir John Fowler. He and Sir Benjamin Baker jointly supervised the erection of this immense structure in steel (Bouch had trusted too much to cast iron for his Tay Bridge), which even today dominates the scene for miles around, though now joined by its more slender road partner. It is 1 mile 1,005 yards long; the approach viaducts contain fifteen main spans and seven arches; 51,000 tons of steel in total were used for the bridge.

Access: By train, the bridge is impressively viewed because of the curvature at the south end, and speed is reduced over the bridge itself. By road, it can be

'Greenwich Time' clock at Waverley Station, Edinburgh

Best seen from the the water's edge, the Forth Bridge is still, after nearly a century, an engineering marvel

well admired from the shores of the Firth or from the A90 which crosses the water via the new road bridge (toll). OS map 65.

Tay Bridge

The longest bridge in Britain (2 miles 50 yards) is also one that, unlike most railway bridges, can be well seen and appreciated as you cross it by train. This is because of the curved approaches, always taken at reduced speed. It is certainly a site not to be missed on any visit to Scotland, partly because of its impressiveness, partly for its tragic history. It is the second bridge on the site, the first Tay Bridge having collapsed on 28 December 1879 in a storm of hurricane force just as a train was crossing the central portion of the bridge. The engine and carriages were thrown into the Firth of Tay below, and all seventy-five people on board were lost. (This disaster is incorporated in A.J. Cronin's well-known novel *Hatter's Castle*, where it is described with considerable accuracy.) The engine, incidentally, was eventually recovered and restored to working order.

Most Victorian engineers built huge safety factors into their structures, by modern standards excessively strict. Their caution has enabled their great bridges to carry vastly increased train loads – more than could possibly have been foreseen at the time of construction – over a century later. Why then was the Tay Bridge an exception? Its designer, Sir Thomas Bouch, had departed from the practices of his contemporaries in some previous bridges that he had constructed by using iron trusses which were cheaper than the alternative materials, and with apparent success. His design for the Tay Bridge, required to carry only a single-track railway, included cast-iron columns supporting the bridge girders, instead of solid brick piers. The bridge rose towards the central section to obtain the clearance demanded by the Admiralty of seventy-nine feet above high-water level; this section was carried on larger structures known as the 'high girders', which contrasted with the apparently flimsy approach girders.

The appalling disaster of the collapse shocked the nation. Poor Bouch was disgraced and the plans he had already prepared for a Forth Bridge were immediately abandoned. The enquiry into the catastrophe concluded that his Tay Bridge had been 'badly designed, badly constructed and badly maintained'. This blow almost certainly led to Bouch's early death. But the Victorians were not easily defeated and a Bill for a second Tay Bridge – the present one – was obtained less than twelve months after the disaster.

The bridge one sees today is built alongside the old one, whose piers (a tragic reminder) can still be seen just above high-water level. There was of course no question of using cast iron in the new bridge's construction: it stands on massive brick foundations and carries a double line of railway. The high girders in the centre are composed of 245-foot and 227-foot trusses. It does not convey quite the same impression of enormous strength the Forth Bridge does, but it has stood for a century, successfully withstanding the tremendous gales

The Tay Bridge, seen from the Dundee end; it is the longest bridge in Britain

that sometimes beat along the Firth of Tay in wintertime – a tribute to engineering persistence in combating Nature's worst moods.

Access: As already suggested, the bridge can be well viewed from a train. By road, there are various approaches along the shores of the Firth, on each side, from all of which a fine impression can be gained. OS map 54 gives several choices.

Perth Station

This station has always been a frontier point between the Lowlands and the Highlands. This frontier character it shares with Carlisle; its architecture also has a strong affinity with that of the English station. Three railway companies used to join at Perth in its ownership and use: the Caledonian, the Highland and the North British. The station (and also the adjacent Station Hotel) was managed by the Perth General Station Committee who appointed the stationmaster, sometimes from some 'neutral' railway to avoid any danger of favouritism in the station operating.

As a gateway to the Highlands Perth Station was often congested with traffic, especially at the opening of the grouse-shooting season. The refreshment room, a noble apartment with a panelled ceiling, Corinthian columns and huge marble fireplace, recalls those days; it was traditionally renowned for the variety of whiskies it stocked.

The station was designed by 1847 by Sir William Tite, and extended in 1865. The style is perhaps less Scottish Baronial than Tudor. The fine circulating area, with its lofty glass arched roof, was always adorned with floral hanging baskets in summer, a delightful practice which the Caledonian Company followed at a number of its stations.

The adjacent Hotel, built in matching architectural style, formerly owned a notable collection of coats-of-arms of the pre-grouping railway companies on panels displayed in the covered way, now removed, that led from the station to the hotel foyer. These have now been transferred to the National Railway Museum at York.

Dalmally Station

Dalmally is a charming and typical Callander & Oban Railway station, dating from 1880. It stands on that part of the line which survives though now connected to the West Highland line at Crianlarich, instead of to the former Caledonian main line at Dunblane.

The station house is in red sandstone with 'crow-stepped' gables and a very ornamental platform awning.

Dalmally Station, typical of the Callander and Oban Railway

Inverness Station

Inverness Station has long shared with Limerick Junction in Eire the distinction of being one of the very few stations which trains enter backwards! It is really two termini, whose platforms adjoin at the buffer-stops and are served by a joint concourse. History, as usual, is the reason. The Inverness & Nairn Railway, later absorbed by the Inverness & Aberdeen and then by the Highland Railway, built its first terminus in Academy Street in 1855, on a curve leading south. Later, the Farther North line was initiated by the Inverness & Ross-shire Railway, which reached Dingwall in 1862. A through station was very difficult to plan; it would have involved a complete removal of the existing terminus. So, although a through avoiding line was built, the Farther North trains were brought into curving platforms which form the apex of a triangle.

In order to facilitate passenger interchange between the Perth and Aberdeen routes on the one hand, and the Farther North line on the other, trains that are continuing beyond Inverness run past on the direct line and then reverse into the station, alongside a train for other destinations.

The River Ness Viaduct just outside the station at Inverness, a fine ashlar sandstone work

Inside the triangle was formerly sited the Lochgorm locomotive works of the Highland Railway, which not merely repaired but also built some locomotives for the Highland Railway, though the majority were purchased from outside builders.

Outside the station's light and spacious concourse, in the open square of Academy Street, its façade is matched by the 1855 Station Hotel in a French-Italianate style (Scottish Baronial might have been more appropriate!) and also the later Highland Railway's head office building, dated 1873-5. The company's former board room is handsome and has a finely decorated ceiling.

Inverness: Clachnaharry Swing Bridge

The Caledonian Canal, one of the only two canals owned by the State before nationalization of the waterways in 1948 (the other was the Crinan Canal, also in Scotland), was intended to link the Atlantic Ocean and the North Sea and thus save shipping the stormy passage through the Pentland Firth. It was never used as expected and, in fact, was always a financial burden on the Treasury. However, in the eyes of the Admiralty it had potential strategic value, and when the Inverness & Ross-shire Railway built its line out of Inverness, great care had to be taken to avoid obstructing the canal where the railway crossed it. A swing bridge solved the problem of maintaining a clearance for shipping without raising the railway too high.

The first bridge, built in 1862, was replaced in 1909 by the present structure, of similar design. It crosses the canal at a skew angle and is a bowed box-girder construction, forty-two yards in length. Formerly a small station stood here, where tickets were collected on southbound trains approaching Inverness. There is no station now, but a signal-box on the north side of the bridge protects the railway when the bridge is opened.

O.S. Nock tells a story about the Duke of Sutherland, a Director of the Highland Railway who was also a great railway enthusiast (see under Dunrobin Station, p.192). He had his own locomotive, a small tank engine which he greatly enjoyed driving. One day when the bridge was open and signals were at danger, along came the Duke's saloon with His Grace driving the locomotive at a spanking pace; a belated full brake application just, and only just, halted the engine by the signal. The stationmaster (who also had charge of the bridge) thereupon gave the Duke a stern dressing-down for 'dangerous driving'. The Duke took it in good part, even though it came from one of his own employees.

Clachnaharry Swing Bridge over the Caledonian Canal – seldom opened for the Admiralty!

Access: Trains from Inverness to all stations north pass this bridge. By road, leave the city centre by Academy Street, joining the A9 for the River Ness and the canal crossing. OS map 26.

Glenfinnan Viaduct

The combination of sharp curvature and low speed sometimes enables train passengers to obtain a good view of railway works of interest along the line they are travelling. (A world-famous example is the great Horseshoe Curve on the former Pennsylvania Railroad near Altoona, USA.) The Glenfinnan Viaduct on the West Highland Extension Line from Fort William to Mallaig must be one of the most-photographed of all railway structures, whether from the ground or a moving train.

It is a Grade A listed building, standing at the head of Loch Shiel, close to the column erected to mark where Bonnie Prince Charlie raised his standard for the abortive 1745 rebellion. The viaduct, curved throughout in a graceful arc, has twenty-one spans and is 516 yards long, blending magnificently with the wild landscape. It is relatively modern, having been built in 1901 for the Mallaig line's opening.

Access: By train, Fort William to Mallaig. By road, on the A861, Fort William to Lochailort. OS maps 40 and 41.

Connel Ferry Bridge

Though nowadays exclusively a road bridge, since closure of the railway branch to Ballachulish, this splendid structure crossing an arm of Loch Etive is well worth visiting. It is notable on scenic as well as engineering grounds, since it spans the Falls of Lora, where the waters rush most impressively below. The Caledonian Railway in 1903 bridged this inlet of the sea with a viaduct on the cantilever principle, wide enough to accommodate both road and rail traffic.

But while the canny railway company had calculated that road traffic would pay tolls sufficient to help pay for the construction cost, the equally canny local authority declined for some considerable time to agree the proposed scale of charges; so it was several years before road-users were able to share the bridge with the trains. For a time too, the Caledonian Railway insisted that motor vehicles be run onto flat wagons and hauled across the bridge by a motor tractor with flanged wheels running on the railway track. Eventually a more sensible course was adopted: raising and adapting the bridge floor so that road vehicles could drive across under their own power. When this was done, the roadway had to be closed by gates at each end before a train could be signalled through.

The superbly-curved viaduct at Glenfinnan is one of the most spectacular Scottish railway structures

The viaduct is unusual in that the uprights of the two cantilevers incline inwards towards the centre of the bridge. There is a height above high-water mark of fifty feet, and a clear span of 500 feet. The engineer was H.M. Brunel.

Access: Junction with the A85 Crianlarich–Oban road, to the A828 signposted Ballachulish, about 2½ miles before reaching Oban. OS map 49.

Dunrobin Station

Unlike some of their English counterparts, most nineteenth-century Scottish aristocrats and clan chieftains welcomed the coming of the railway, which offered a prospect of reviving areas that had been depressed ever since the Rebellion of 1745. The savage repression that had followed, with the break-up of the clans, the reduction in croft farming and large-scale emigration to Canada, the United States and elsewhere, had left a depopulated countryside. Enlightened landowners saw new rail communications as opening the door to a better life, as Macpherson of Cluny envisaged in his address at the ceremony of cutting the first sod of the Inverness & Nairn Railway in 1854.

The Duke of Sutherland even built his own railway for some seventeen miles from Golspie to Helmsdale in 1870. His seat was Dunrobin Castle, about two miles north of Golspie. His railway was operated for some time by a single locomotive and a few coaches of his own, until in 1871 the Highland Railway (formed by a process of amalgamations in 1865) took over the train working.

A station for the Duke of Sutherland's railway was built in 1870 at Dunrobin, and it was used by Queen Victoria two years later when she visited the Duke. It was rebuilt in 1902, to the design of the architect to the estate, L. Bisset. This private station is a little half-timbered building with three gables, completely charming. Formerly trains called there for ordinary passengers only with the Duke's permission.

Successive Dukes of Sutherland were Directors of the Highland Railway and, after 1923, of the London Midland & Scottish Railway. Their tradition of enthusiasm for railways was inherited, and at Dunrobin Station a tiny engine shed long housed a small tank engine privately owned and sometimes driven by a duke. Like many American businessmen, the family also had its own private railway saloon carriage and, even in LMS days, this was attached to ordinary trains, on request, for the Duke's journeys south. The saloon was lent by the Duke to King Edward VII and Queen Alexandra for a train journey from Invergordon to Ballater (for Balmoral) in 1902. Rather

The Duke of Sutherland's private engine 'Dunrobin' and his private saloon

sadly, on nationalization this agreeable relic of feudalism was brought to an end. The Duke was informed that BR would not continue to haul his saloon as heretofore, and he thereupon decided to sell it. Happily, the station building has been the subject of recent restoration, and excursion trains from Inverness, Aberdeen and Edinburgh call there during the summer by arrangement between BR and the Sutherland Trust.

Access: Dunrobin station building is on the private estate of the Duke of Sutherland, on the north shore of the Moray Firth between Golspie and Helmsdale. The A9 trunk road passes. OS map 17.

Ballater Station (closed)
The first railway along Deeside was promoted by a small independent company called the Deeside Railway. However, it had difficulty in raising the funds for construction and was taken over by the Aberdeen Railway Company in 1848. The line thereafter was opened in sections as far as Aboyne; the last stretch from Aboyne to Ballater was built by

Thurso Station has an all-over roof, very suitable on the cold shore of the Pentland Firth

the separate Aboyne & Ballater Railway and opened in 1866. These small railways were merged in the Great North of Scotland Railway in 1876. The line was closed by BR in 1965.

Ballater, as the railhead for Braemar (and thus for Balmoral Castle), has always been a station of interest. In Queen Victoria's time it was served by special 'Queen's Messenger' trains from Aberdeen, bringing the Queen's despatches and papers from London – even running on Sundays when the rest of the railway was virtually closed down. These trains were revived for King George V after 1919 (the King did not visit Balmoral during the war years) and only finally disappeared in 1938.

The station was never very elaborate, just a single-storey wooden building and a glass platform awning, but behind the *porte-cochère* there was a royal waiting-room, used on the occasions of Queen Victoria's twice-yearly visits to Balmoral and also of the countless journeys of European royal personages and other important visitors, such as Prime Ministers, who came to Balmoral on political business or social occasions.

The station is now used as an information office for tourists and also a restaurant.

Access: By road only, the A93 from Aberdeen to Ballater. OS map 44.

Thurso Station

About twenty miles west of John O'Groats is Thurso, the most northerly railway station in Britain, looking out over the Pentland Firth to the Orkneys with their Scandinavian affinities. The railway station was built in 1874, by the Sutherland & Caithness Railway (later absorbed by the Highland). As befits this bleak coast, it is cosy and squat, with a wooden roof covering the train shed and platform. The station offices are in a single-storey stone building with round-headed windows and a projecting gable. The building material is sandstone rubble.

With the use of Scapa Flow as a great naval base, Thurso became of great importance in the First World War, being the nearest railway station. Daily special trains were run for Navy personnel between London and Thurso (717 miles), covering the journey in $21\frac{1}{2}$ hours. This practice revived during the Second World War to a considerable extent.

Curiously, at the southern extremity of Great Britain, the nearest railway station to Land's End, Penzance, also has an all-over roof and train shed, with a modest stone station building.

Appendix: The Railway Preservation Societies

A quarter-century ago, few people could have forecast the astonishing growth of the movement for the preservation of sections of railway by private societies of enthusiasts. The movement had two principal origins. One was a desire to resuscitate a section of railway (usually in an attractive area of countryside) and operate it for the pleasure of railway buffs and tourists; the other was the ambition of restoring particular steam locomotives which had been displaced by diesel or electric traction and which were awaiting breaking-up, having been sold by British Railways to a scrapyard.

There are at the time of writing no fewer than sixty-three full members of the Association of Railway Preservation Societies, and an even larger number of associate members. The preservation societies vary widely in their scope and constitution. BR's all-Region timetable gives particulars of train services regularly operated by a number of private railway companies. Some maintain attractive and/or historic buildings, as well as locomotives and rolling stock. There is, however, space to mention here only some of the most notable preserved systems. There are books giving much fuller details.

One point to be borne in mind is that 'restored' stations are sometimes the result of a sort of 'cannibalization' process; for instance, a signal box or footbridge of a suitable type may be purchased, dismantled and re-erected at another station at which a preservation society is trying to re-create the right period and character of a past railway system.

The preservation movement really started in the 1950s with the steps to re-open the Ffestiniog Railway which, despite being a narrow-gauge line (1 foot 11½ inches, or 597 mm, track gauge), has probably the best claim to be the most 'historic' of all the preserved systems. The original Ffestiniog Railway Company was incorporated by Act of Parliament in 1832, only a couple of years after the opening of the Liverpool & Manchester Railway. So the company is well over

150 years old; it has retained its identity throughout that period, unlike most of the early railways which were amalgamated or absorbed into bigger systems.

The Ffestiniog Railway was built to link the slate quarries around Blaenau Ffestiniog with the little port of Porthmadog, a distance of over thirteen miles; originally it was operated by horse traction, and for freight only. The slate trains ran down to the port mainly by gravity, with the horses, which hauled the empty wagons back to the quarries, riding in 'dandy carts'.

In the 1860s steam traction was introduced and passenger services started. Soon the line was operated by the unique 'Fairlie' double-bogie articulated steam locomotives, which proved very suitable for the steep gradients of the line, some being built in the railway's own workshops at Boston Lodge, just outside Porthmadog.

The railway's history became complicated and its prosperity declined towards the end of the nineteenth century. After the First World War financial problems continued; passenger traffic ceased at the outbreak of the Second World War, and all traffic ended in August 1946.

The long struggle to revive the railway started in 1951. From 1954 onwards, the work of reinstating the track progressed by stages, with passenger services in the tourist season gradually extending from Porthmadog, first to Boston Lodge, next to Minffordd, then to Tan-y-Bwlch. At this stage, unfortunately, the construction of a new reservoir submerged part of the original route to Blaenau Ffestiniog.

A prolonged legal battle over compensation followed, with a final award of £106,000 – inadequate to meet the cost of the new railway which had to be constructed, including a difficult tunnel and a remarkable spiral curve. Finally in 1982 Blaenau Ffestiniog was reached once more, and the Ffestiniog Railway joined British Rail in a new station there.

About the time (1955) when work on reinstating the Ffestiniog Railway had commenced, the Southern Region of British Railways decided to close the East Grinstead to Lewes line, locally nicknamed the 'Bluebell and Primrose line'. But the closure was challenged in the courts by a local landowner, Miss R.E.M. Bessemer (a great-granddaughter of the inventor Sir Henry Bessemer), because the original Act of 1878 authorizing construction had required the provision of a train service in perpetuity (four trains each way daily). British Rail was forced to restore the train service until, $2\frac{1}{2}$ years later, new Parliamentary powers had been obtained that authorized the closure.

This episode was given wide publicity both locally and nationally.

Minffordd Station: attractive architecture on Britain's oldest narrow-gauge working railway

In 1959 a preservation society was formed to take over the 4½ miles of railway from Horsted Keynes to Sheffield Park and operate a steam-hauled service as the 'Bluebell Railway'. For the last quarter-century the society has progressively extended its activities, including the complete restoration of many steam locomotives and passenger coaches. No fewer than twenty-six locomotives and thirty-four coaches (including an observation and a Pullman car) are in stock.

In addition, Sheffield Park Station has been lovingly restored to LBSCR condition and is a fine period piece. Horsted Keynes Station – an impressive affair for a country branch line, with four platforms – has also been restored, but to the standards of the later Southern Railway.

The Bluebell Railway was a pioneer in its field, and it also set an example by being run on business lines. Its success prompted other schemes. The Severn Valley Railway was the most prominent project of the next decade. The railway had originally opened in 1862 and linked Hartlebury with Shrewsbury, via the picturesque town of Bridgnorth. It was taken over by the Great Western Railway in the 1870s and closed, in instalments, by BR in the later 1960s, ending in 1970.

To counter the closures, the Severn Valley Railway society was formed in 1965 and enthusiastically supported by the late Sir Gerald Nabarro MP. It gradually accumulated the resources to acquire and re-open the line from Bridgnorth to Bewdley; in 1984 a link with BR at Kidderminster was also opened. Today the SVR is one of the largest and most successful of the preserved railways – nearly sixteen miles of route, eight stations, over thirty steam locomotives and more than half a dozen diesels. It is run on extremely professional lines. Added to that, it traverses some beautiful scenery, following a river valley not served by a road and thus offering exceptional views by train. Bridgnorth, the northern terminus, is a town of great interest and character, with the river valley separating the High Town and Low Town areas.

The buildings most worthy of note are some stations, especially Arley, Hampton Loade and Bridgnorth, and the fine Victoria Bridge over the Severn just south of Arley, designed by the famous engineer Sir John Fowler in 1861. It is a graceful ironwork arch with a 200-foot span.

The character of this preserved railway is as close to that of the former Great Western Railway as possible. Even more 'Great Western' is the Dart Valley Railway which comprises two former GWR branches: from Totnes on the main line as far as Buckfastleigh, and from Paignton, the present terminus of the BR Torbay line, as far as Kingswear. The Totnes-Buckfastleigh line (formerly continuing to Ashburton) had been closed under the Beeching regime and was re-opened in 1969 by the Dart Valley Light Railway Company on a commercial basis as a tourist attraction, the opening ceremony being performed by Dr (by then Lord) Beeching himself, who remarked that had he not closed the line he would not have been able to re-open it! The stations have been restored entirely in character.

The Paignton–Kingswear line was taken over, by arrangement with British Rail, immediately on withdrawal of the BR service in 1972. Its official title is the Torbay & Dartmouth Railway and it is of 'main line' character, in that through excursion workings from British Rail are operated from time to time. Kingswear Station is the embarkation point for the ferry to Dartmouth.

Film and television viewers who enjoyed *The Railway Children* will recognize many scenes on the Keighley & Worth Valley Railway, a privately preserved line that runs from Keighley to Oxenhope.

Devotees of the Brontë family's novels will regard Haworth, which is an intermediate station on the line, as being of special importance. The station of principal architectural interest is Oakworth, maintained as nearly as possible in its original Midland Railway condition. It won first prize in the Best Preserved Station competition in 1979. The headquarters of the railway, however, is at Haworth, where most of the rolling stock is maintained.

During the 1970s a major success story in the railway preservation saga was the Mid-Hants Railway, or 'Watercress Line'. Its origin was a single-line cross-country route from Alton to Winchester built by the Mid-Hants Railway Company in the 1870s. It was worked from the outset by the LSWR, which in 1884 bought up the independent company. The main object in building this small railway, about nineteen miles long, had been to improve communications in a wholly rural area, the only industry of importance being the extensive watercress beds around Alresford which led to the railway being nicknamed the Watercress Line, a name which has stuck.

However, it had a second and occasionally very important function: when the main line was closed, either on account of an incident or for major maintenance, traffic between London, Southampton and Bournemouth could be diverted via the 'Watercress Line' or, as railwaymen used to put it, 'over the Alps' on account of the severe gradients between Alton and Alresford where the line traverses the Hampshire uplands.

The line was closed in 1973 on grounds of economy, but a preservation society had already been formed; after long negotiations with British Rail and the local authorities involved, the section of line between Alresford and Ropley (three miles) was eventually acquired, and a number of locomotives and carriages were made available to operate trips by 1977. Station buildings were also renovated and the line was extended as far as Medstead and Four Marks, and later to Alton, $10\frac{1}{2}$ miles in all, for steam trains. At Alton there is cross-platform interchange with British Rail's electric trains to and from Waterloo.

Other preserved railways over which regular train services are operated in the summer months include the Strathspey Railway from Aviemore to Boat of Garten where the latter station has been lovingly reconstructed. At Grantown-on-Spey, seven miles further on, the station, which is a particularly fine example of Highland Railway architecture, is being preserved by the Regional Council.

The West Somerset Railway is actually the longest section of privately preserved railway in the country, almost twenty miles in length and with nine passenger stations. It runs from Bishop's

Alresford Station has been carefully restored in many LSWR details by the Mid-Hants Railway

Lydeard to Minehead, where the station is almost on the sea-front.

Mention should also be made of the Nene Valley Railway, part of the former Peterborough–Northampton line, closed to all traffic in 1972. In 1977 the Peterborough Railway Society was able to open about five miles of line from Wansford to Orton Mere, beyond which there is an end-on connection with British Rail. Stations have had to be rebuilt, but to a very simple standard. The headquarters of the line is at Wansford, where the locomotives and rolling stock are housed. The only surviving original feature of Wansford Station is the very handsome 1845 Tudor-style building, built for the London & Birmingham Railway, the architect being J.W. Livock, sold by BR when the line was closed and now used as offices. It has splendid gables with spiked finials, and the frontage is in local stone, matching the village architecture.

Lastly, one 'light railway' must be mentioned. Britain was slower than many European countries to develop light railways in order to improve communications in agricultural districts at relatively low cost. However, in 1896 a Light Railways Act was passed with this object in view, and several lines were promoted. The first to be built was the Kent & East Sussex Railway, linking Headcorn in Kent with Robertsbridge in Sussex, a distance of twenty-one miles, serving only one town of any size, Tenterden, *en route*.

The promoter was Lt.-Col. H.F. Stephens, who controlled a group of light railways – mostly financially unsuccessful – for some thirty years. He died in 1931. The railway continued to operate independently, however, until it was nationalized in 1948. British Railways progressively withdrew first the passenger and then the freight services, but in 1973 the Tenterden Railway Company Ltd was formed to take over as much as possible of the line and reinstate it from Tenterden Town to Northiam.

As already mentioned, the main object of many societies is the restoration to working order of redundant steam locomotives. As thousands of these were displaced in the 1960s, their largest single graveyard was Messrs Woodhams' scrap depot at Barry in South Wales. The merchant was shrewd enough to realize that purchasers could be found for a number of locomotives not as scrap metal but for restoration. Unfortunately, raising the necessary funds for purchase often proved a protracted business – and the cost of restoration could also be alarmingly high, especially when engines had been exposed to the weather for years.

However, a number of voluntary organizations have rescued and restored many locomotives which can be steamed from time to time, even if substantial train services are not operated. Centres of this activity include the East Somerset Railway at Cranmore Station, the Didcot Railway Centre, the Midland Railway Centre at Butterley in Derbyshire, the Yorkshire Dales Railway at Embsay, near Keighley, and the Isle of Wight Railway at Haven Street Station.

If the restoration of locomotives and rolling stock to service is usually the first priority of preservation societies, it is nevertheless very gratifying that the restoration of stations and structures is often a very close second objective. British Rail in fact presents an annual award for the best-preserved station in private ownership. In many cases, restoration has been difficult because over the years a station may have suffered from under-maintenance as traffic fell off. One answer has been to purchase redundant structures such as signal-boxes that are of the right company origin and period, dismantle and remove them to a 'restoration' site. The Midland Railway Trust purchased a complete closed station – Whitwell – took it down and re-erected it at the Trust's headquarters, Butterley, where it could not possibly look more authentic! The original train shed at Edinburgh (Haymarket) was transported to Bo'ness by the Scottish Railway Preservation Society.

As a counterpart to the preserved and re-opened sections of railway, there are of course permanently abandoned lines, often shown on Ordnance Survey maps as dotted lines marked 'Course of old railway'. It will be realized that these are *no* evidence whatever of the existence of a right of way. But there is a growing amount of interest in exploring disused railways.

The attitude of local authorities to establishing paths for walkers, cyclists and riders along closed railway lines has often been unsatisfactory. BR has been under a statutory obligation after a rail closure, to offer the land to the local authority – but only for a short time, which is usually insufficient for a bureaucracy to make up its mind about alternative uses, to formulate a plan and get it approved. There are also other factors at work: possible agricultural or industrial uses and the disposal value that British Rail can realize. Obviously, in principle, it would be better, before any line is closed, if firm arrangements could have been made for the future use of all the land thus made available; it would have avoided the process of piecemeal disposal that has too often been the sequel to a closure. But the pressures have been great, and result is that too few closed railways have been opened to walkers, cyclists and riders. Where access *is* possible, detours around tunnels, closed sections and broken bridges may be inevitable. Even so, public interest has produced many plans for extending the paths that already exist. Readers who wish to take up this activity – which can soon grow into a hobby – may consult the books listed under 'Further Reading'.

Acknowledgements and Further Reading

First, I must express my deep gratitude to British Rail, both to the Director of Public Affairs at headquarters and to numerous BR Regional and Area officers who have unearthed photographs for this book.

I am also greatly indebted to London Regional Transport, to the National Railway Museum in York, the Science Museum in London and several public libraries, museums and individual photographers and collectors. They are too numerous to list individually here, though picture credits are of course given.

The total number of books about railway engineering and architecture is so huge as to make selection extremely difficult. Much information about the history of individual stations and structures can often be gleaned from railway histories that are not primarily concerned with buildings or architecture. But pride of place must go to *The Railway Heritage of Britain*, by Gordon Biddle and O.S. Nock, published by Michael Joseph and the British Railways Board in 1983.

Much information about London Transport stations can be obtained from *The History of London Transport*, by T.C. Barker and Michael Robbins, a definitive work published by George Allen & Unwin.

A useful compendium of information about the preserved private railways is *Railways Restored*, published by Ian Allan. Two books suggesting itineraries for walkers along disused railway lines are *Walking Old Railways*, by Christopher Somerville and *Railway Walks*, by Gareth Lovett Jones, both published by David & Charles; and those interested in the minutiae of railway archaeology can usefully consult *Railway Relics*, by Brian Morgan, published by Ian Allan.

An exhaustive railway bibliography is available in the Library of the Chartered Institute of Transport, as well as various public libraries, for those who wish to pursue detailed research. Primary sources can often be unearthed in local history sections of public libraries.

Index

Individual sites are listed under the following headings: bridges, hotels, museums, stations, tunnels, viaducts.